The E
Through H

The Beatles Through Headphones

The Quirks, Peccadilloes, Nuances and Sonic Delights of the Greatest Popular Music Ever Recorded

TED MONTGOMERY

McFarland & Company, Inc., Publishers

Jefferson, North Carolina

Library of Congress Cataloguing-in-Publication Data

Montgomery, Ted, 1958–
    The Beatles through headphones : the quirks, peccadilloes, nuances
and sonic delights of the greatest popular music ever recorded / Ted
Montgomery.
        p.   cm.
    Includes bibliographical references and index.

    ISBN 978-0-7864-7863-7 (softcover : acid free paper) ∞
    ISBN 978-1-4766-1701-5 (ebook)

    1. Beatles.   2. Rock music—1961–1970—History and criticism.
I. Title.
    ML421.B4M65 2014
    772.42166092'2—dc23   2014025494

British Library cataloguing data are available

The Beatles: Ringo, John, George and Paul in the studio, 1967
© Apple Corps Ltd./Photofest

Printed in the United States of America

McFarland & Company, Inc., Publishers
  Box 611, Jefferson, North Carolina 28640
    www.mcfarlandpub.com

For my own Fab Four:
Vicki, Kyle, Kelly and Sean

Table of Contents

———————

Table of Contents

Acknowledgments

—————

No author creates a work of this length in a vacuum. Time and space do not permit me to adequately express my gratitude to the dozens of individuals who supported me while I wrote this book, but several are worthy of particular mention.

Many friends encouraged me, directly and indirectly. Dave Groves patiently listened as I endlessly extolled the drumming virtues of Ringo Starr. Dave's a drummer, and that argument doesn't also resonate with every drummer, but Dave was a good sport about it.

Katie Williams conducted vital research for me, and helped to track down the quotes that are scattered throughout the text.

Kevin Knapp, who has written about rock and roll music for several publications, happily engaged me on a variety of Beatles-related topics, and gave me good insights on some of the earliest pages I had written.

Mark Nowlin is a lifelong friend who nurtured my love of the Beatles during our schooldays and beyond. Mark knows as much about the Beatles as anyone I know, and acted as my chief sounding board throughout the writing of this book.

One friend, Al Shippey, is no longer with us, but his impact is felt throughout these pages. Al and I spent 30 years playing and singing Beatles songs together, and much of the musical language I have access to is by dint of my friendship with Al.

Many other lend their support by quietly rooting for the project from the sidelines. Special thanks to Leon Frasson, Debra Lashbrook, Kathleen Wiles, Shelby Olsen, Lillian Lorenzi, Geoff Upward, Mike Dubin, Lois Hunter, Ellen Byerlein, Dan Bodene, Danielle Dimcheff, Mary Micallef, Yvonne Pappas, Jake Alverez and Elena Godin.

My family supported me throughout. Barbara Montgomery, Janis and Carmen Verde, Linda and Brad Harding, Cindy Montgomery, Dan and Patti Montgomery, Lindsay and Jason Harding, Joshua Verde and Elinor, Peter and James Montgomery were all four-square in my corner as I endeavored to create this book.

My wife, Vicki McNiff, and stepkids Kyle, Kelly and Sean McNiff, gave me a wide berth in a small space because they knew how passionate I was about this project. Their love and support was essential to the success of this project. Joey Shada, too.

Finally, it seems rather gauche to write acknowledgements for a book about the Beatles and not give John Lennon, Paul McCartney, George Harrison and Ringo Starr full credit. Their music has played a paramount role in my life, and I'm grateful I got to listen in.

Preface

———

This is a book about the music of the Beatles. It is also a book about listening to their music in a different way.

No other catalogue in popular music is as revered and cherished as the music the Beatles recorded and released between the end of 1962 and the beginning of 1970. Indeed, no other catalogue has influenced more musicians or had such widespread cultural impact as the Beatles'. We're still talking about it, parsing and listening to the music more than 50 years after it was created.

Perhaps no other popular cultural icons have had more published works devoted to them than the Beatles. Books about the band number in the hundreds, and include everything from insider looks from producers and engineers, to slightly revisionist hagiographies from those with only peripheral connections to the Beatles' inside circle. Fans have written books about their favorite Beatles songs, and disc jockeys and other music industry nabobs have penned fond remembrances based on their own experiences. There are even a few books in circulation that are critical of the band and its music. Such has been the epic sweep of the cultural swath the Beatles cut through the 1960s.

I grew up in a suburban Detroit home with three older sisters firmly in the thrall of the hometown hit-making machine known as Motown Records. The 45s that enjoyed heavy rotation on my sisters' record players tended to be the hits that Berry Gordy's stable of talent turned out seemingly every other week: the Supremes, the Four Tops, the Temptations. The first rhythm section I heard did not include Paul McCartney and Ringo Starr; it was Benny Benjamin and James Jamerson.

Even though I was very young during the 1960s, I was aware of the constant thrum of pop music that wafted down the hallway. Still, I don't remember hearing the Beatles in our home.

I didn't "discover" the Beatles until after they had broken up. My best friend and I—totally fascinated by all the colorful gingerbread that graced the covers of *Sgt. Pepper* and *Magical Mystery Tour*—started listening to their records and quickly became infatuated with the sound collages and interesting harmonies the band created. To me, it sounded like no other pop music I'd ever heard.

I had a lot of catching up to do. I never got to hear a "new" Beatles album as it was coming out; their entire output was in millions of homes before I even discovered the band. Over time, I collected the entire catalogue (on vinyl, of course) and my love of Beatles music began to breathe with an energy that seemed exciting and invigorating.

One summer during the mid–2000s, I thought it might be interesting to listen to the Beatles' entire catalogue on headphones. As this endeavor progressed, I started taking notes on what I heard that I didn't recall hearing over external speakers. The sonic landscape on the headphones was rich with mumbled utterances by the band members, broken guitar solos buried deep in the mix, odd meter mishaps and other delightful ear candy that wasn't obvious if you listened in your car or on your stereo system.

Around this time, I teamed with a professor—a true Beatles scholar—at the university where I worked to lead a weekly Beatles discussion. I was struck by the number of college-age students who came to these discussions; most of them hadn't yet been born on the day John Lennon was murdered.

At this same time, portable digital music players became the main conduit through which we listened to our music. Now, everyone was on headphones (or earbuds). I wondered if anyone else interested in Beatles music was hearing the same things I heard.

Thus, the idea for this book was born.

I spent literally hundreds of hours with headphones strapped to my head, listening and re-listening to everything the group recorded. I was amazed at the things I began to hear that I never really noticed before.

At times, it was tedious work; listening to a song like "Don't Pass Me By" or "Maxwell's Silver Hammer" over and over again demands a certain monkish fealty to the subject at hand. Those moments were tempered by the exquisite and sublime experience of hearing the band rip through the near flawless "All My Loving" or the heady "You're Going to Lose That Girl."

This book is not a biography of the Beatles, nor does it purport to offer an extensive review of their music (although because it examines the Beatles' catalogue in chronological order, it does suggest a certain historical trajectory). The main purpose of this book is to help the reader discover a certain untapped sonic clarity in the recordings and to uncover some of the hidden nuggets that I contend the Beatles purposely planted deep in the mix of their songs.

This book is not laden with quotes or specious ruminations of the sort found in Wikipedia biographical sketches. It is truly the work of a Beatles devotee who believes that he has brought forth something new from listening to the greatest popular recordings of the twentieth century—on headphones.

To fully understand what we will discuss in this book, it is necessary to use a pair of high-quality headphones, and to make sure you put them on properly. Most high-quality headphones have each can labeled "left" or "right." If you put them on incorrectly, you'll hear the sounds described in this book on the opposite side of where they were intended to be in the stereo spectrum. They should fit comfortably and completely over your ears. For my comprehensive review of the Beatles' catalogue, I used a pair of Sony MDR-V600 dynamic range stereo headphones.

Earbuds, omnipresent in this day of digital music players, are insufficient for the purposes of understanding what's in this book. They often don't fit in the ear properly, and they are notorious for significant sound leakage. Listening to the Beatles' catalogue on earbuds is akin to watching an opera on your smartphone.

A large portion of this book is personal examination on the author's part of how the songs sound through headphones. The book contains opinions and critical exposition on what can be discovered by listening to the Beatles' music through headphones. Consequently, most of the book does not require footnotes or attributions. In the few instances where attribution is necessary, you will find the appropriate source citation in the endnotes. The author culled some of this material from interviews with the former Beatles and their circle of producers and engineers.

It's important to note that the Beatles themselves are poor chroniclers of their own history. Many of the things they've said in interviews are simply untrue, and are likely products of the fallibility of human memory, and the mixing of fact and myth that occurred as a natural byproduct of the constant scrutiny they received from the press and biographers. And, while they always publicly evidenced a jaundiced eye toward the less than savory biographies written about them that emerged over the years, it's clear by careful examination of their statements that they had at least a casual familiarity with what was written about them.

I will also attempt to expose some long-held myths about the recording of the music. There are many books written by Beatle insiders that are considered definitive texts on the recording of the Beatles' canon: George Martin, Mark Lewisohn, Geoff Emerick, Ken Scott and others have authored books about recording the Beatles, and their recollections and detailed analysis must be taken seriously. However, I think in a very few cases, their observations are wrong. While I was not privy to the masters of the Beatles' recordings while writing this book (as many of the aforementioned insiders were), I nevertheless can draw conclusions from a close listen to the Beatles' catalogue that refute some of their assertions. The best example of this is "Eleanor Rigby." While Lewisohn and others wrote that Lennon and Harrison sang backing vocals on this song, I contend that all of the vocal parts were sung by Paul McCartney. You just can't hear Lennon and Harrison when you listen to "Eleanor Rigby" on the headphones. The remixed version of the song that appears on the *Love* album only serves to strengthen the argument that McCartney was the sole singer on that song.

I'm aware of the hubris contained in this statement. How can someone who wasn't there dispute the words of those who were? For our purposes in this book, we will examine only what we can hear on the headphones, and not what was logged on the tape boxes. In the case of "Eleanor Rigby," there is simply no audible evidence of Lennon and Harrison singing on that track.

Such assertions are, of course, anathema to Beatles purists who cleave to the generally accepted lore about the group. The passage of time and the handing down from generation to generation of the folklore associated with the Beatles has certainly muddled some of the facts.

You've probably spent most of your time listening to the Beatles over a stereo system with external speakers. Their music sounds wonderful this way, of course, but this way of listening to the group does not deliver the full sonic picture of what the Beatles created. To come to a full appreciation of their craft and artistry—to say nothing of their innovation—one must listen carefully to their entire catalogue over high-quality headphones.

The Beatles—especially Lennon and McCartney—were fascinated by sound and every possible manipulation of it. Early on in their recording career, they were more or less captive to the production sensibilities of their label-assigned producer, George Martin, but as their popularity (and power) grew, they began to spend more time exploring new sounds and incorporating instruments into their songs that heretofore hadn't played a role in the creation of rock music.

They were pranksters, too. Their music is rife with double entendres, cheeky sexual innuendo and sly references that could make the most precocious schoolboys howl with delight. As time went on and they became more seasoned recording artists, they actively sought to imbue their music with interesting little sonic tidbits that can only be heard on headphones. This was heretofore unique in rock and roll up to that time, but soon became commonplace as other artists came to admire the beautiful aural pictures the Beatles were painting in the studio.

The Beatles themselves spent a large chunk of their recording lives with headphones strapped to their ears. The process of overdubbing, of course, requires that the singer or player hear what he's singing or playing over. While they were the creators of every sound to be heard in their catalogue, it would be surprising if even they were aware of some of the things that have been discovered in this comprehensive review of their musical *oeuvre*.

This book will explain in great detail the nuances and quirks to be found in a close-up listen to Beatles music. Mistakes, studio corrections, mumbled phrases—the Beatles music is a sea of sonic delights and peccadilloes. The author's goal is to give each reader a new and enlightening perspective on the greatest popular music ever written, performed and recorded. As a bonus, the reader will get a brief but incisive review of every song the Beatles ever committed to tape.

So strap your headphones on and try to hear it my way.

Part One

The Band

Terms and Equipment

Throughout this book, a few technical terms are frequently used. What follows are brief definitions of these terms:

- Artificial Double-Tracking (ADT): The process of taking one recorded track (usually a vocal track) and feeding the signal through a second recording device, then rerouting it back to the original source. By superimposing the second signal on top of the original and slightly altering its timing, the effect creates a fuller sound with just a slight delay. This technique, especially favored by John Lennon, made it unnecessary to re-record an identical vocal track, thereby speeding up the recording process and giving the vocal a meatier, punchier sound. You will see as we discuss the middle period of Beatles recordings that they used ADT quite often, and usually to great effect. This step in the recording process long ago was made obsolete by the development of software recording suites like ProTools.

- Stereo spectrum: This refers simply to the placement of sounds in the stereo picture. From the bottom left of your headphones to the bottom right, and all places in between.

- Panning: Panning refers to the process of moving a sound in the stereo spectrum either to the left or right.

- Potting: Potting refers to the movement of the volume level of each instrument and voice in its track position. Engineers can either "pot" up or down each individual track to achieve the desired decibel level.

The CD Catalogue

No rock and roll band's catalogue has been more zealously guarded by its keepers than the Beatles'. They resisted until the eleventh hour making their catalogue available through iTunes (ostensibly because they had an ongoing lawsuit over the trademark Apple that was the mark for the Beatles' record label and the distinguishing mark of Steve Jobs' Macintosh computer line).

When the Beatles' entire catalogue was first released on CD in 1987, it created the expected stir in music circles. For the first time, the greatest catalogue in popular music could be heard on the supposedly pristine compact disc format.

Unfortunately, the albums were not remastered, and consequently suffered from a sound that was muddy and uninteresting. The fact is, the original vinyl albums sounded clearer and jumped out of the speakers with a more urgent sonic clarity than the 1987 CD releases.

This problem was rectified with the 2009 release of the entire CD catalogue, this time completely remastered by a team of engineers at Abbey Road studios. The team was careful not to diddle with the mixes, but in effect "washed" the master tapes to strip them of the detritus that had built up on them over the decades.

The effect was astounding. Acoustic guitars came alive with a new shimmer, electric guitars were crunchier and janglier, and the bass—notoriously insufficient in many Beatles recordings—found a new prominence in the remastered set. Even the drums sounded heavier and punchier.

It is strongly recommended that you listen to the 2009 remastered Beatles' catalogue rather than the 1987 release.

A Short History

They were improbable saviors of culture, Western thought, style and most of all, popular music. Never before had anyone from the working class port city of Liverpool, England, made an impact on any of those things. Liverpool produced its share of locally popular comedians, dissolute chroniclers with a decidedly hangdog outlook on life. But the city never made an impact on the world. That is, until the early 1960s. The sound emanating from that northern industrial port city would be felt throughout the globe.

Liverpool lies 220 miles northwest of London, but the two cities might as well be on different continents for all their differences. London, the economic and cultural hub of England in the 1960s (and still today), prides itself on being a gateway European destination for tourists from all over the world. Its restaurants, cultural attractions and historical pedigree are the pride of all Londoners, who seem imbued with a certain provincial snootiness that tacitly lords it over the rest of England.

Liverpool in the 1960s, on the other hand, had long suffered from a civic inferiority complex that is betrayed by an air of defensiveness subtly emanating from its citizens. Proud, hard working and hard-living, Liverpudlians of the era were content to stay in their own sooty backyards rather than sully themselves with the well-known economic and social excesses of the London power elite.

Onto this backdrop burst four young men in their early 20s, with guitars, matching suits and haircuts that were outlandishly girlish for the times (although quite conservative by today's standards).

These four lads had something else, though. Their quirky physical appearance aside, they possessed a gift for writing and singing pop songs with memorable melodies, totally innovative harmonies, and musical hooks that quickly captured the collective consciousness of the listening public. Moreover, they were given to frequent declarations of honesty and irreverence when speaking in public, something their more measured and reticent pop brethren rarely felt secure enough to do. Finally, Liverpool had some native sons of which to be proud.

All four Beatles were born within a span of three years in the first part of the 1940s. John Lennon was born on October 9, 1940, right around the time that Hitler's Luftwaffe was strafing Liverpool. His mother was unable to care for him, and entrusted his upbringing to her sister. Lennon's father was not a part of his life. Ringo Starr was born on July 5, 1940, in the poorest part of a very poor city. His father was gone forever within a year of his birth. Paul McCartney was born on June 18, 1942, to a mother who was a nurse at the local hospital, and a father who toiled for 40 years in a cotton mill, but spent his evenings playing in pubs as the leader of the locally popular Jim Mac's Jazz Band. George Harrison was born on February 25, 1943, to Harold and Louise Harrison. Harrison's dad was a bus driver.

The humble beginnings of the four Beatles gave them the intestinal fortitude they would need to soldier on in the midst of the chaos they would encounter in the ensuing years, and enabled them to stay as normal as possible, at least in the context of rock stars. (This humility and these strong family values were passed on to the children of the Beatles. None of the Beatles' children have ever been in any public trouble. No tabloid coverage of drug busts, drunken nightclub melees or domestic abuse for the Beatles' kids.)

Still, it is wholly inaccurate to say the Beatles grew up in abject poverty, which is the mythic story often told in biographies about the band. None of the Beatles' families were wealthy, to be sure, but all four of the boys always had clothing, food and shelter, and were educated in the manner to which all lower-middle class British boys were accustomed.

Lennon and McCartney, the most successful songwriting duo in the pantheon of popular music, both lost their mothers at early ages. Lennon's mother was run down by a drunk driver when he was 18, and McCartney's mom died of breast cancer when he was 14.

In many ways, Lennon and McCartney were opposites. Lennon was sardonic, cynical and always cast a jaundiced eye toward the world around him. McCartney's personality was sunny, his outlook positive; he was the consummate PR man, and knew how to glad-hand the press contingent at the ubiquitous press conferences.

Perhaps because of their opposing natures, a winning songwriting formula was struck. This is encapsulated in two of their best songs. In "We Can Work It Out," McCartney the optimist sings the title words while Lennon chimes in with a caveat. In "Getting Better," McCartney again sings the title lyrics while Lennon's words sting.

Harrison played a key role early in the band's career by bringing to the mix the signature Beatles guitar sound that informed almost all of their earliest songs. Understandably cowed by the superlative songwriting and singing talents of Lennon and McCartney (not to mention their outsized personalities and egos), Harrison eventually gained the confidence to start bringing his own compositions into the studio for consideration. And while many of these early efforts were weak affairs, Harrison eventually evolved into a good songwriter and singer, and surreptitiously used the rift that was growing between Lennon and McCartney as a springboard to improve his own station within the band, and his reputation among his rock and roll peers.

Starr at first played the role of lovable clown to a rapt audience of teenyboppers and their mothers. He seemed like the least significant member of the group in the early days, but that image belied his important contributions to the overall sound of the band. There couldn't have been a better drummer for the Beatles than Ringo Starr.

What is most amazing in retrospect is that none of their albums sound like the album before. This is unprecedented in rock music during their era. The Beatles definitely had a style all their own, but they built on it with each album and made sure not to repeat themselves.

The Beatles were responsible for many innovations that we now take for granted today. Remind yourself that at the time the Beatles made the scene, pop music was populated by groups whose lead singer was the focus: Buddy Holly and the Crickets, Frankie Valli and the Four Seasons, Bill Haley and the Comets. Go ahead and name one Cricket, Four Season or Comet. Yet, John, Paul, George and Ringo nearly became one word in the lexicon of the 1960s.

Not only did "John, Paul, George and Ringo" become part of our language, but many of their song titles have been repurposed for use in newspaper and magazine headlines, and even use in everyday conversation. "The Long and Winding Road" is often used as a metaphor for an arduous journey, and "Ticket to Ride" has been used as slang for being granted the freedom to travel. "Magical Mystery Tour" is often used in reviews of movies, stage shows and popular music. "We Can Work It Out" has been used as a headline in news stories with subjects as serious as the leaders of nations at war coming to a grudging detente, and as trivial as a celebrity couple deciding to get back together again after a nasty and public divorce, separation or falling out. The Beatles—through their music—created a wholly novel lexicon that has firmly insinuated itself into our everyday language.

Conventions that we take for granted—lyrics printed on the album, gatefold albums, rock videos and many other innovations—were minted by the Beatles. At a time when Elvis Presley was making the same movie over and over again, the Beatles were producing thoughtful, frolicsome and significant rock and roll movies that forever exiled films like "Beach Blanket Bingo" to their own special level of cinematic purgatory.

Some of their innovations were less successful: Apple Records, one of the first-ever record labels started and owned by an artist, was a noble effort based on a magnanimous desire to provide a creative outlet for talent who lacked the necessary industry connections. James Taylor, Mary Hopkin, Badfinger and Jackie Lomax were some of the artists discovered by the Beatles who went on to varying degrees of success. When the Beatles tried to extend their largesse by creating clothing store and electronic subsidiaries of their label, they quickly found themselves out of their realm. They were artists and not businessmen. Eventually, the enterprise collapsed under its own weight.

By today's standards, "I Want to Hold Your Hand" sounds amateurish and tinny from a purely sonic standpoint. This was due in part to the technological limitations of the era. Still, it is necessary to cast yourself back in time to fully understand the phenomenon that the Beatles fomented. There was simply nothing at all like it being played over the airwaves at the time. Such rock luminaries as Bob Dylan, Neil Young, Tom Petty, Bono, and many others point to February 7, 1964, the date on which the Beatles first appeared on *The Ed Sullivan Show*, as the moment that they decided to become rock stars.

Perhaps our sons and daughters don't realize this, but nearly every song they listen to today is somehow derivative of the Beatles' output. Their impact on popular music is so deeply entrenched, that it is well nigh impossible to write a pop song today that doesn't refer to a Beatles song in some way.

The Beatles' recording career was neatly encapsulated in just eight short years. When they officially broke up on April 10, 1970, it somehow seemed fitting that they handed over the torch to others as a new decade began. They were definitely a product of the 1960s.

The Beatles took an existing musical genre—rock and roll—and redefined its parameters. Emboldened by their abiding love of their most influential forbears—Buddy Holly, Gene Vincent, Carl Perkins, Little Richard, Elvis, the Everly Brothers—they took rock and roll to new heights of innovation, complexity and gravitas. Rock and roll, in their hands, suddenly became an essential art form, much to the dismay of the starchier cognoscenti of popular culture.

The Beatles accomplished all this in a few short years. Their friends and rock compadres, the Rolling Stones, continue touring and recording 50 years on, but it's been at least a couple of decades since they made memorable music. The rock and roll band career arc just isn't designed for the long haul.

Lennon-McCartney

To assert that John Lennon and Paul McCartney forged the greatest popular music songwriting partnership in the twentieth century is akin to saying that the laws of gravity will never be repealed. The impossibly obvious thesis inherent in that statement cannot be refuted by logical argument, nor can it be disproved by a priori evidence. Lennon and McCartney authored the finest catalogue of music created in the twentieth century. It's that simple.

To be sure, they came along at precisely the right moment. The pop landscape of the early 1960s was littered with songs chiefly authored by songwriters who were not members of the groups who made them famous. Mike Leiber and Jerry Stoller were churning out radio-ready hits for Elvis Presley, and the Brill Building roster of Gerry Goffin and Carole King, Ellie Greenwich and Jeff Barry, Burt Bacharach and Hal David, Barry Mann and Cynthia Weil, and Doc Pomus and Mort Shuman were supplying numerous groups with accessible pop that has definitely stood the test of time.

Lennon and McCartney were the first songwriting partnership to actually produce hits for their own band. To underscore how novel an

13

approach this was at the time in pop music, one only has to consider the fact that George Martin actively campaigned to have the Beatles record other writers' songs in an attempt to get off the ground as a band. Luckily, the Beatles resisted this ploy (although they did record many cover versions of songs they admired written by other songwriters).

It's impossible to know for sure how Lennon and McCartney came by their incredibly innate ability to write radio-ready pop songs of lasting significance and overwhelming influence. It might be enough to say that genius in any field is inborn, and not learned. In other words, the gifts were already there; they just needed an outlet.

John Lennon was mainly influenced by Gene Vincent, Eddie Cochran, Elvis, and a host of Motown and Stax artists. He also loved moderately obscure R&B artists like Larry Williams and Arthur Alexander. His writing tendencies leaned heavily toward the earthy, organic rock and roll that paved the way for countless other artists to expand on.

Paul McCartney favored Little Richard and Elvis, but also had a keen fondness for the Everly Brothers, whose close harmonies and acoustic-based pop heavily informed the earliest Beatles albums. McCartney was also interested in show tunes and light jazz, an outcropping of the influence his father—who fronted a jazz band that played standards and apparently accentuated the schmaltz level of some of those tunes—had on him as a boy. You can't write "When I'm Sixty-Four" and "Honey Pie" if your only frame of reference is Little Richard.

The songwriting partnership really flowered during the time the band was cutting its teeth by touring England and Hamburg, Germany, in the early 1960s. Stuck in countless traffic jams in a van on the motorway, or confined to a dingy motel room in some God-forsaken northern European outpost, the acoustic guitars invariably came out to while away the long hours. Sitting knee-to-knee, Lennon and McCartney found the chemistry—borne of a shared enthusiasm for the songs of their key influences—to craft near-perfect two-minute pop songs rife with melody, harmony and hooks. The formula coalesced, and the pop music universe was forever realigned.

Once the duo had experienced significant success churning out hits, the partnership began to unravel ever so slightly. Although they had an agreement to label any song written by either partner a Lennon-McCartney composition, both writers often came up with their own songs and, through force of habit, previewed it for the other, with the vague hope that a suggestion might improve the song. Indeed, this happened often.

By the time *Help!* came out in 1965, most of the songs on that album credited to Lennon and McCartney were written by one or the other. Obviously, Lennon had nothing to do with the writing of "Yesterday," and McCartney had no hand in composing "You've Got to Hide Your Love Away."

This arrangement worked well. The royalties rolled in, and both Lennon and McCartney enjoyed their growing reputation as the greatest songwriting duo in pop music.

Right up until *Revolver*, John Lennon was in full control as the putative leader of the band. His songs dominated the first five albums, and the sixth album—*Rubber Soul*—found Lennon at the peak of his abilities as a lyricist and singer. It wasn't until they recorded *Revolver* that Paul McCartney began to exert his considerable talents as a composer and singer. The last six albums are heavy with McCartney-penned tunes, and he seems to have been leading the group in terms of album strategy and direction. McCartney seemed to have grabbed the helm, and the others more or less went along with the new band leadership paradigm.

Later, petty skirmishes occurred about who wrote what, with the authorship of songs like "Eleanor Rigby" (McCartney) and "In My Life" (Lennon) particularly in question.

It seems that Lennon and McCartney paid scant attention to George Harrison's output. For the early albums, they'd either write him a song to sing, or allow him to cover a song by one of his musical heroes. Later, when Harrison's songwriting talents blossomed, he was definitely a force to be reckoned with, and room had to be made on each album for his work. From *The Beatles* (*The White Album*) forward, Harrison's compositions at least approached the quality of the Lennon-McCartney writing machine. Indeed, an argument could be made that "Something" and "Here Comes the Sun" are the two best songs on *Abbey Road*.

Both partners brought their unique gifts to nearly every Lennon-McCartney composition, if only by dint of their playing, singing and random studio suggestions. McCartney didn't contribute a thing to the writing of "The Ballad of John and Yoko," but his bass, drums, piano and harmony vocal added a lot to its sound. Likewise, Lennon didn't help write "Get Back," but his lead guitar and harmony vocal gave the song an extra lift. There are countless examples of this, especially from 1967 through 1970.

Much has been made over the years of the fractious relationship between McCartney and Lennon, and it is true they began to go their separate ways, starting in 1967. But you can still hear both men working hard to make the other's songs sound as good as possible. They clung to the core ideals of their original songwriting partnership, even in the late stages when the Beatles' ship began to take on water. For all their subsequent sniping about who wrote what, it's clear that both men always held the other's work in high regard.

Their final five studio albums contained hardly any song-writing collaboration, but the credited partnership remained intact. Today, the Lennon-McCartney songbook is considered sacred musical text in the world of popular music.

The Recording Process

The recording process that George Martin and the Beatles employed evolved over time on a continuum that closely followed the contour of their creative arc. As their creativity and innovation blossomed, so too did the intricacies of their recording technique. They were constantly looking for ways to add more interesting sonic colors to their music, and leaned heavily on Martin to help them realize their vision.

On their first album, almost all of the instruments and vocals were recorded live. Since they only had two tracks to work with, there were very few overdubs, and those that did occur were done as corrective measures rather than to sweeten the track. Curiously, they did not fix every mistake (see the discussion of the stereo version of *Please Please Me*). Basically, when the red light went on in the studio, the Beatles played their songs (almost all of which had been staples of their live act for years) in a rote performance that required little in the way of retakes.

The next four albums saw the band using more in the way of instrumentation and elaborate harmonies, which required Martin to be more inventive to achieve the sound they were after. This was the period during which they began to have access to four-track recording consoles.

From *Rubber Soul* onward, the recording studio became somewhat of a sound laboratory, with the mad scientists mixing and matching potent combinations of sound that forever changed how bands make the best, most innovative use of the recording technologies available to them.

The process was fairly simple at first. A click track was created, which established the time signature that the band was to play to. Think of a click track as a metronome, creating a precise beat so each member of the band could play in time with each other.

Over the click track, the drums, guitars and sometimes the bass would be recorded. Because they had so few tracks to work with, Martin would often bounce (or ping-pong) a finished track to an empty track, thereby clearing a track for more recording. In this way, they would have guitars, drums and bass all on one track, with room enough on the three remaining tracks for vocals and more instruments. The downside to this technique was that none of the instruments on the bounced track could be separated from each other. When mixing for mono, this didn't present much of a problem, but later on when stereo mixes were the goal, this was a thornier issue.

The bouncing process was not without its risks. The track that was to be bounced had to be considered a "good" take, because once it was bounced, it had to be used in the final mix. If a fatal mistake was discovered in the bounced track upon subsequent listens, the only choice was to scrap the entire track and start over.

Also, bouncing a track created another generation, and sonic quality erodes with each new generation of the original recording.

The next step was usually the creation of a "guide" vocal, a vocal track that was not necessarily considered a finished take. This allowed the band to refine the vocals as the recording session progressed, and to add appropriate harmonies, if so desired. The last recording step was the addition of extra percussion, handclaps, or other instruments (typically keyboards). Often, the original bass part was wiped so that McCartney could lay down a fresh (and more inventive) bass part that more closely matched the spirit and tenor of the finished song. The click track was also wiped once it had served its purpose.

The Beatles Anthology presents an instructive look into their recording process. There are two working versions of "Eight Days a Week" on the *Anthology* that show the Beatles trying to establish the harmony vocals, and the way in which George Harrison's electric guitar should sound. Both versions are quite a ways away from what they eventually released, but it's fascinating to hear them on their journey.

The *Anthology* also includes an interesting early take of "Got to Get You Into My Life," with just an organ, spare drums and acoustic guitar, plus McCartney's guide vocal and backing vocals from Lennon and Harrison that were finally scrapped. Listening to this version of the song, and what they eventually released, is an incisive look into the evolution of a Beatles song. How they created an up-tempo rocker with funky horn charts from the rather tame early version is further testament to their creativity and desire to constantly stretch their musical sensibilities.

Finally, the working version of "And Your Bird Can Sing" that is on the *Anthology* shows Lennon and McCartney trying to perfect a song they don't sound like they believed was a great piece of work. Over two electric guitars, bass and drums, plus harmony vocals that were previously recorded, Lennon and McCartney try to add two more vocal parts, but end up convulsing into spasmodic laughter that is either a product of their exhaustion or their cannabis intake, or both. That they eventually scrapped the entire basic track they had created and started recording the song from scratch demonstrates their commitment to always releasing a quality product.

In the early years, the guys stayed down on the studio floor, rarely if ever venturing into the control room, which was strictly considered George Martin's domain. They entrusted him to capture the right sound, and to manage his team as they engineered, mastered and mixed the finished tapes until there was an end product: the album (or single) itself.

During the mixing process, effects were added to the instruments and voices. The most common effects used by the Beatles were reverb, echo, compression and phasing. John Lennon was particularly fond of echo and reverb and would often ask George Martin to apply these effects to his vocal while he was recording it, rather than later during the mixing process. Lennon used the reverb and echo on his voice as a sort of rhythmic device to lay down the best vocal possible. If Lennon's vocal was particularly good, Martin would sometimes remove the effects during the mixing process.

The effects they used were essentially vocal sweetening effects. Today, of course, Auto-Tune is ubiquitous in pop, rock, country and rap music. However, Auto-Tune is an effect that was originally created as a pitch correction device. If you removed the Auto-Tune effect from many of today's country music singers' voices, you would likely immediately notice some pitch problems. Generally speaking, the Beatles didn't have pitch issues.

The question about whether the Beatles would have used Auto-Tune if it had been available to them is an interesting one. It's likely they would have dabbled with it, and one can envision John Lennon especially having a brief fling with the device. Lennon was the Beatle most interested in the manipulation of the sound of his voice, and it's likely he would have found Auto-Tune briefly fascinating as a studio effect. But in the end, the Beatles would have likely abandoned Auto-Tune when they realized that it created a fake vocal track by correcting the singer's faulty pitch. It is not to be considered on a par with echo and reverb, which give vocals a bigger and wider sonic quality, but do nothing to correct faulty notes.

As the Beatles grew more powerful (and more demanding), they made forays into the control room and eventually garnered a significant say in how the songs were mixed.

Later on, when strings and horns were commonly used in the Beatles' recordings, Martin acted as musical interpreter for the group's very precise specifications, since their limited musical lexicon prevented them from talking in the same language as an experienced concert or session musician.

On *Sgt. Pepper's Lonely Hearts Club Band*, they started using odd musical effects (comb and paper, bubbles blown into a container of water, etc.) that required still more room among the traditional mix of rock and roll instruments. Factor in the orchestra used on "A Day in the Life," and you can begin to intuit the recording challenges that faced George Martin.

That the Beatles got such a huge sound on *Sgt. Pepper* using just four tracks is a recording achievement of epic proportions. One can only imagine what they might have produced if they had had access to today's recording technologies.

Sir George Martin

No serious discussion of the Beatles music would be complete without including Sir George Martin, their first producer, mentor and musical translator.

At the tender age of 24, he was hired at EMI, England's largest and most prestigious recording label. This was a fortunate turn of events for both Martin and the Beatles, who were still 12 years away from coming into his orbit.

By the time Martin met the Beatles, in 1962, he was chiefly a producer of comedy albums for EMI, running tape for such comedy luminaries as Peter Sellers. The Beatles' manager, Brian Epstein, had brokered a meeting with Martin to try to get the Beatles an audition with a major label. Martin had no experience recording pop music.

To his credit, he saw something in the Beatles that was palpable and engaging. He intuited their obvious energy and collective force of personality, yet was savvy enough to recognize the group didn't yet have the musical chops necessary to record. There was a lot of work to be done.

At first, Martin tried to determine which Beatle should be the leader of the group. Pop groups at the time were almost always led by the main singer, and the members of the group backing the singer were fairly anonymous.

He naturally gravitated toward John Lennon, who at the time was the putative leader of the Beatles and possessed the strongest personality. But before too long, he recognized that the other three had distinct, appealing personalities in their own right. Over time, he abandoned the idea of anointing one Beatle as the leader.

Initially, the Beatles were in awe of Martin. His impressive musical pedigree, the proper suits he wore, and the manner in which he carried himself were enough to keep the group in his thrall. Martin called all the shots in the studio early in their career, and the Beatles didn't dare seek an audience with him in the control room.

Over time, as the Beatles matured and their music demanded more innovative instrumentation and edgier recording techniques, Martin became more of an adviser than bandleader. The Beatles—none of whom could read or write music—relied on him to notate on staff paper the sounds they had roiling around in their heads. Martin's contributions during the middle period of the group's career included scoring the strings on "Yesterday" and "Eleanor Rigby," and playing the piano solo on "In My Life."

Martin also appeared surprisingly often as a musician on Beatles recordings, especially in the very early years. A talented piano player in his own right, he sat in on many of the band's early recordings, such as "Not a Second Time," "A Hard Day's Night" and "Money," among many others. That he was able to so easily adapt to a rock and roll style of playing when that style clearly was not his forte shows his nimbleness as a musician. It also indicates that he did not yet trust Lennon and McCartney to deliver the goods on piano.

In the early period, Martin's stereo mixes of Beatles songs were not very inventive; typically, all the vocals were on one side of the stereo spectrum, and all the instruments on the other. Over a car radio, this sounded fine. On headphones, it can sound bland and almost funereal.

For all his talents, Martin had some limitations. He never really got a sustained and shimmery acoustic guitar sound, at least in the early days. He allowed Starr's incessant riding of his cymbals to produce an annoying and persistent hiss on some of the earlier songs. And most egregiously, he didn't figure out how to record and mix a bass track with any oomph until much later in the band's career.

Martin can be forgiven for much of this; this was the prevailing mix strategy of the day in pop music. Moreover, EMI at the time had strict specifications on how much bass and treble could be applied to recordings. Later, as the Beatles wandered off into the artistic ether created by the use of substances and the adoption of a "love is all you need" ethos, his mixes became more interesting and inventive.

It must be noted at this point that stereo recordings were never the original goal of Martin and the group. Stereo was still a relatively new innovation in the early 1960s, and not even on Martin's radar screen. He mixed the Beatles sound in mono, because that was what he had to work with at the time.

Martin was certainly astounded by the big leap in the Beatles' creativity that spawned the ground-breaking work on *Rubber Soul, Revolver* and *Sgt. Pepper's Lonely Hearts Club Band*, but he also sensed that they were breaking from his tightly controlled studio etiquette. They'd sneak off to the studio's bathroom to have a quick marijuana break, hoping that Martin didn't catch them in the act. At this point, Martin morphed from musical director to hall monitor, at least in their minds.

It was McCartney who relied on Martin more than the other Beatles. McCartney's music was always more music hall inflected, and his interest in symphonic music was not shared with the same enthusiasm by Lennon and Harrison. Martin translated McCartney's ideas into arrangements for the French horn solo in "For No One," and the piccolo trumpet in "Penny Lane," to name just two examples of his deft melding of pop music and classical instrumentation.

By the time the Beatles came back from India and started work on the *White Album*, group infighting and musical disagreements created obvious splinters in the band's cohesiveness. Martin left much of the production work on that album to his young protégé, Chris Thomas. The *White Album* is notable for its almost complete lack of production.

Likewise, during the recording of *Let It Be*, Martin was barely involved. It was only when the Beatles set about making their farewell album—*Abbey Road*—that Martin exerted himself once again. His production fingerprints are all over *Abbey Road*, and helped make the album a beautiful coda to the Beatles superlative career.

Martin had lots of help in the studio. Geoff Emerick, Chris Thomas, Norman "Hurricane" Smith, Ken Scott and many others twiddled the knobs under Martin's direction, and all played a vital role in creating the Beatles' music.

George Martin's contributions to the Beatles' sound cannot be overstated. He took an unknown group comprised of raw talent, harnessed their energy and exuberance, and helped mold them into the most innovative recording artists of their time. He was their liaison to the world of sound production and classical instruments, and he translated their musical ideas into wholly creative records. That their music is still frequently played today is a tribute to Martin's production taste and sensibilities. He was the perfect producer at the perfect time.

The Beatles as Musicians

Virtually no one regards the Beatles as the best rock musicians of all time. They were certainly very competent, and they did create an overall sound that has been copied and envied by future generations of rock musicians. But strictly from a virtuoso standpoint, none of the Beatles were considered complete masters of their respective instruments, with the undeniable exception of Paul McCartney and his bass playing.

John Lennon was the rhythm guitarist, one of the most important roles in any rock band. His style was understated and workmanlike. Especially during the early years, his guitar drove the band and provided an underpinning of rhythmic urgency. Listen to his acoustic guitar work on some of the early ballads ("And I Love Her," "If I Fell" and "I'll Be Back," to name a few) to get a good sense for how his rhythm work was an essential part of the band's overall sound. On some of his more up-tempo songs ("Help," "I'm a Loser"), Lennon's acoustic guitar is the instrument driving the rest of the players.

On the few occasions when Lennon played lead guitar ("Roll Over Beethoven," "You Can't Do That" and "Get Back"), he produced elliptical solos that were perfect for the songs.

In later years, he seems to have had a reduced role in the overall instrumental sound of the band. On *Sgt. Pepper* and *Magical Mystery Tour*, Lennon's guitar playing is often either missing entirely or relegated to a minor role in the overall mix. He does play a lot of guitar on *The White Album*, and employs a new picking technique that he learned while the band was in India (listen to "Dear Prudence" and "Julia" for good examples of this technique).

His keyboard playing is simple, relying on elemental chording and very few fancy flourishes. It usually shows its hand as a complement to some of their earlier rock and roll songs ("I'm Down" and "Kansas City/Hey Hey Hey Hey"). From *Magical Mystery Tour* through *Let It Be*, Lennon only rarely played keyboards on Beatles' songs, that chore having been almost entirely ceded to Paul McCartney.

McCartney is generally regarded as the best—and most innovative—rock and roll bass player of all time. He first picked up the bass in

Hamburg, Germany, after the untimely death of the band's first bass player, Stuart Sutcliffe. The chore was given to him by default; Lennon and Harrison wanted nothing to do with learning the instrument. Always willing to have a go at something new, McCartney mastered the bass and turned it into something more than just a subtle complement to the band's rhythm section. From *Rubber Soul* on, McCartney's bass informs nearly every Beatles song with a low end that is a signature part of their overall sound.

Later on, from *Sgt. Pepper* through *Let It Be*, McCartney is the dominant keyboard player for the band. His keyboard style is wholly inventive (listen to "Martha My Dear" or "You Never Give Me Your Money" to get a sense of his keyboard prowess). On *Abbey Road*, he plays bass and keyboards on almost every track.

His acoustic guitar playing is wildly underrated. Listen to "Yesterday," "I'm Looking Through You," "Blackbird" and "Mother Nature's Son," and you'll get a sense for his acoustic guitar prowess.

On the few occasions when McCartney assumed the lead guitar role, he acquitted himself well. "Ticket to Ride" and "Taxman" stand out chiefly because of McCartney's electric guitar solos.

On a very few occasions, McCartney sat in for Starr on the drums. "Back In the U.S.S.R.," "Dear Prudence" and "The Ballad of John and Yoko" all feature McCartney on skins.

Harrison is the Beatle whose instrumental prowess improved the most from the early days of the Beatles right through Harrison's solo career. Known for his great love of Carl Perkins and James Burton, most of his early solos were new takes on rockabilly and country and western lead guitar conventions ("Everybody's Trying to Be My Baby," "Honey Don't" and "I Don't Want to Spoil the Party"). Almost every time Harrison strayed from the comfort zone created by his guitar heroes, he played something memorable that stood out as among the best rock and roll guitar solos of all-time ("All My Loving," "Can't Buy Me Love," "I Saw Her Standing There"). Later on, his solos became much more fluid and melodic ("Something," "Let It Be"). It was only during his solo career that he developed his talent on the slide guitar, a sound for which he is now known.

Harrison's acoustic guitar work is vastly underrated, mostly because he didn't play the acoustic guitar very often in the band. Listen to "Here

Comes the Sun," "For You Blue" and "Long Long Long" for key representations of his best acoustic guitar playing.

Starr's drumming has been much maligned over the years, but this is completely without merit. While he didn't employ the drum god histrionics favored by contemporaries such as John Bonham and Keith Moon, his playing was always in the pocket and always complemented the song. Listen to "She Loves You," "Ticket to Ride" and "Day Tripper" for great examples of innovative drum playing that doesn't overwhelm the great songs they support. Later on, Starr's work on *Revolver*, *Sgt. Pepper* and *Abbey Road* was uniformly stellar.

The Beatles as Singers

Any intelligent examination of the individual Beatles as singers shouldn't only focus on their individual voices and styles, but must also include a discussion about how their groundbreaking harmonies forever changed rock and roll music.

It's important to remember that at the time the band broke on the music scene, most groups had one lead singer. The Beatles had two from the start, and George Harrison eventually emerged as a competent vocalist in his own right. This was heretofore unprecedented in early 1960s rock and pop.

John Lennon and Paul McCartney developed their vocal chops by playing eight-hour gigs in the seedy Hamburg nightclubs that gave rise to their burgeoning talents. Hoarse from too much drink, too many strong European cigarettes, lack of sleep and the obvious wear and tear that anyone's vocal cords would endure from eight-hour sets, Lennon and McCartney were still able to coalesce their vocal talents into a unified sound that merged the deep soulfulness of Lennon's voice with the clear tenor of McCartney's.

The signature sound of what we all regard as the Beatlemania period is not the ringing electric guitars, the in-the-pocket drum parts or the incessant handclaps that were omnipresent on the earliest records. No. It's the joyous sound of the harmonies, developed by Lennon, McCartney and Harrison on stage and in the studio.

"I Want to Hold Your Hand," "She Loves You," "This Boy," and countless other early songs were identified by and cherished for the inventive block harmonies that gave the Beatles a decided advantage over their contemporaries when it came to capturing the adulation of young fans (both girls *and* boys). Check out the old concert footage; invariably, it's at the precise moment when the three Beatles' voices merge in perfect harmony that the girls swoon and scream, and the boys clap their hands together with a vigor that can only be described as maniacal.

The Beatles were aware, at least by 1964, that their singing was what usually brought the house down. Obviously, most of the songs were great; perfect studies in economical pop craft, with enough hooks and melodies to get lodged in the music loop of the fans' minds. There was never anything easier to do in this period than to immediately identify a Beatles song by the way the voices jumped out of the car radio.

As the band matured and the focus turned more and more to the lead singer, the ebullient harmonies on the early records morphed into a more strategic and clever arrangement of background vocals. As we examine the albums in greater detail, you'll recognize the precise moment that this change began, and you'll be able to fully chart the serpentine evolution the harmonies underwent as the years went by.

During the middle period—especially on *Rubber Soul* and *Revolver*—there are many songs on which all three Beatles are singing at the same time. However, they seem to have abandoned the harmonic style that infused so many of their earliest recordings.

John Lennon possessed one of the most recognizable and soulful voices in rock and roll history. In the early years, he moved easily from out-and-out shouting ("It Won't Be Long," "Rock and Roll Music," "Twist and Shout") to pop balladry ("This Boy," "I'll Be Back," "Yes It Is"). During the middle period, Lennon verged closer and closer to a confessional style of singing ("You've Got to Hide Your Love Away," "I'm a Loser," "In My Life") as he slowly became enamored of studio trickery and tape speed variations that altered the sound of his voice.

Lennon, more than the others, was fond of using reverb and echo to give his vocal more breadth and a certain rhythmic cadence as he sang in the studio. After *Sgt. Pepper*, he used reverb and echo far less often.

In the later period, his songs were equally divided between blues-inflected rock singing ("Happiness Is a Warm Gun," "Yer Blues," "Come Together") and contemplative acoustic singer-songwriter types of compositions ("Julia," "Cry Baby Cry," "Across the Universe"). As we'll note later, his songwriting output (and in some cases, quality control) fell off a bit during the later period. This seems to be related to his growing dissatisfaction with being a Beatle than any sort of erosion of his considerable talents.

Paul McCartney was the lead singer less frequently during the early days, but when he got the chance to rock out, he invariably delivered ("Long Tall Sally," "Can't Buy Me Love," "I'm Down"). By the middle period, he was showing a predilection for acoustic-based ballads ("Yesterday" being the most obvious example of this). He also started getting into writing and singing pop songs that used chamber music and symphonic instrumentation ("Eleanor Rigby," "For No One," "Penny Lane").

In the later period, McCartney continued to show a surprising fondness for hard-edged rock ("Helter Skelter," "Back in the USSR," "I've Got a Feeling"), but would also frequently relapse into his cheesier guise as an out-of-time crooner ("Honey Pie," "Maxwell's Silver Hammer," "When I'm Sixty-Four"). For all his vocal eccentricities, McCartney was probably the most nimble of the Beatles' lead singers, at least in terms of stylistic range.

George Harrison was a less gifted singer than Lennon and McCartney, and during the early days, especially, Harrison was more apt to be heard singing harmonies than lead. His early forays as lead vocalist ("Don't Bother Me," "You Like Me Too Much," "I Need You") were weighed down by his bland, underdeveloped songwriting chops and plain vanilla singing style. It was only when covering others' songs that Harrison seemed to take control ("Roll Over Beethoven," "Everybody's Trying to Be My Baby," "Devil in Her Heart").

During the middle period, Harrison became infatuated with Eastern music ("Love You To," "Within You Without You," "Blue Jay Way"), although on occasion he could deliver a rousing vocal ("Taxman"). During the late period, Harrison vacillated between standard rock styles ("While My Guitar Gentry Weeps," "Savoy Truffle," "I Me Mine") and sweet, highly melodic songs ("Something," "Here Comes the Sun," "Long Long Long"). While not the most gifted singer in the band, his voice lent a certain indefinable quality to the Beatles' overall sound.

Ringo Starr was not a good singer by any measure. Still, when the band gave him the vocal spotlight in the early days, he often delivered a folksy vocal with a winsome quality ("Boys," "Matchbox," "Honey Don't"). The middle period saw Starr handling the vocal chores on some of the band's most popular songs ("With a Little Help from My Friends" and "Yellow Submarine"), while Starr's vocals on his own compositions ranged from bleakly monotonous ("Don't Pass Me By") to charmingly engaging ("Octopus's Garden"). Still in all, as a singer Ringo Starr is a great drummer.

For all the many musical gifts the Beatles bestowed on us, their cheery, inventive lead and harmony vocals were chief among them. To say nothing of the superlative lead vocals provided by John Lennon and Paul McCartney.

1:27

Throughout this book, you will see references to time marks for particular songs. Often, you will see a reference such as "listen for the second electric guitar to come in at 1:56." This provides a guide to the reader (and listener) to hear what the author is attempting to point out as significant or at least interesting.

Most digital music players have features that show the elapsed time of the song playing, both from a starting point and as a countdown. For instance, "She's a Woman" has an elapsed time of 3:04. On the left of your player, you should see 0:00 as the song begins to play, while the right will show 3:04. The left will end at 3:04 and the right will count down to 0:00. Pretty basic stuff.

As the writing of this book progressed, I began to notice that a lot of significant sonic quirks—coughs, broken vocal lines, drop-outs and more—occurred at precisely 1:27. Out of all the specific time notations I point out in these pages, 1:27 is far and away the most common one at which something interesting happens. It's not even close.

This is hardly on a par with the "Paul is dead" rumor machine, and it may not be significant of anything in particular. It is probably just an odd coincidence. But these are the Beatles we're talking about, and as we know, they were clever and mischievous, and actively sought to infuse their music will thinly coded intricacies. One just never knows what one might stumble upon.

In any case, and at the very least, you will notice a lot of interesting things happening at 1:27.

Part Two

The Albums

Introduction to the Albums

In the following pages, you will find a critical analysis of each Beatles album. For our purposes we will examine only the albums that the Beatles intended for you to hear. Capitol, EMI/Parlophone's American licensee, overreacted to the hype of Beatlemania by clamoring for more Beatles product during the intercessions between official releases, and created several bastardized versions of Beatles albums that often included songs already released and, most shockingly, songs that hadn't yet been released by EMI.

The most egregious example of this is the U.S. release of *Revolver*. That album contains only two songs written and sung by John Lennon, and excludes three Lennon songs that were intended for the album (and which are among the best songs on that album). Instead, Capitol created a pastiche of year-old songs, supplemented by the three Lennon tracks cut from the American version of *Revolver*, to create a tired mishmash non-ironically called *Yesterday ... and Today*.

Meet the Beatles, The Beatles' Second Album, The Beatles Story, Something New, The Early Beatles, Beatles VI, Beatles '65, Yesterday ... and Today and *The Beatles Again* (sometimes referred to as *The Beatles Hey Jude*), while interesting in a nostalgic sense, don't actually exist as real Beatles albums. They were the creation of an overzealous marketing campaign to flood the airwaves with Beatle songs, even when the Beatles had no new product to share with the masses.

Our album overview will only discuss the 13 studio albums the Beatles released as they intended you to hear them, plus three others that are essential parts of their catalogue. It is necessary to handle the catalogue in this manner because it is critical to any meaningful discussion of the arc of their songwriting and recording career.

The Beatles catalogue can be grouped neatly into three separate time periods. The first five albums make up the early years, an era in which Beatlemania blossomed as they conquered the world via an unforgiving and relentless tour schedule. They also starred in two very successful major motion pictures during this period, and spent their studio time refining the magic of their signature sound.

The second period—the middle years—was comprised of *Rubber Soul, Revolver, Sgt. Pepper's Lonely Hearts Club Band* and *Magical Mystery Tour*. This is the period during which they quit touring (after the completion of *Revolver*) and also includes their most creative and groundbreaking work. Drugs played a part in this, no doubt, but they were also mastering the studio and the musical possibilities available to express their very fertile ideas.

The final period—the later years—included *The Beatles, Yellow Submarine, Abbey Road* and *Let It Be*. This period is marked by the creation of some great work, to be sure, but also saw the band members not getting along very well and fragmenting their efforts in the studio.

Compilation albums like the so-called "red" and "blue" greatest hits packages, and the surprising 2000 best-seller *One*, will not be examined because they contain songs that appear on albums we will discuss.

We will examine *Past Masters One* and *Past Masters Two*, because they contain the singles that did not appear on albums and other curios (and include some of their best songs). As a bonus, we will also parse *Love*, the album of mash-ups created as a soundtrack to the very popular Cirque de Soleil show featuring the Beatles' music.

We will look at a limited amount of songs culled from the 1995 release of *The Beatles Anthology*, a hodgepodge of outtakes, alternate takes and demos that is fascinating to listen to and shines a bright light on the group's creative process. We'll only examine the handful of songs that the Beatles wrote but did not officially release, a couple of interesting cover tunes, and the two songs they released 15 years after John Lennon's death, through a recording process that would have made Natalie Cole blush. We won't examine the endless alternate takes of Beatles songs included here, or the countless demos on the set. While it is fascinating to hear Lennon sitting in his living room, working on an early version of "Mean Mr. Mustard" on his acoustic guitar, there is nothing interesting about listening to it through headphones.

We'll compare the differences between the two releases of *Yellow Submarine*; the original that includes one side of George Martin's orchestral compositions, and the 2009 remastered set that includes only Beatles songs. We will also compare the two versions of *Let It Be*: the original 1970 release, and the cleaned up version that includes a slightly different running order that appears on *Let It Be ... Naked*.

Consumers don't really buy albums anymore. On-line music sources like iTunes and Spotify make it easy for listeners to cherry-pick their favorite songs from albums. The idea of an album as a wholly formed piece of art has gone the way of eight-track tapes and cassette players.

That's a shame. An album is a snapshot of an artist in the moment, and a document of artistic, cultural and historical significance. No one understood this better than the Beatles.

When someone mentions the second side ("sides," of course, are now an antiquated term with regard to LPs) of *Abbey Road*, one immediately thinks of the medley of song snippets that the Beatles deftly wove together to create a suite of memorable and moving music. Listening to those songs separately robs them of the clarity and context that the Beatles intended.

The Beatles raised the album to a new art form. Each one of their albums stands as a lasting chronicle of the time in which it was created. And each one sounds completely different than the previous one. That is a remarkable and singular achievement in the annals of popular music.

The Stereo Albums

Please Please Me
RELEASED MARCH 22, 1963

"We were in a recording studio for the first time in our lives, and it was done in twelve hours because they wouldn't spend any more money. That record tried to capture us live, and was the nearest thing to what we might have sounded like to the audiences in Hamburg and Liverpool. Still, you don't get that live atmosphere of the crowd stomping on the beat with you; it's the nearest you can get to knowing what we sounded like before we became the 'clever' Beatles."

—John Lennon[1]

"Those old records weren't really stereo. They were mono records and they were rechanneled. Some of the stereo is terrible because you've got backing on one side. In fact, when we did the first two albums—at least the first album, which was '*Please Please Me*,' we did straight onto a two-track machine. So there wasn't any stereo as such, it was just the voices on one track and the backing on the other."

—George Harrison[2]

Please Please Me was the Beatles' first significant introduction to the music world. It's the soundtrack of a burgeoning Beatlemania, replete with joyous singing and the catchiest musical hooks of the day. After this, there would be no doubt that there was a new order in the realm of pop music. It sounded like no other music available at the time.

Their first album includes three songs, "Please Please Me" "P.S. I Love You" and "Love Me Do," that had previously been released as singles. The other 11 songs on the album were recorded in one frenetic and historic day—February 11, 1963. In a remarkable (and today, unheard of) turn-around time, the album was recorded, mixed, mastered, packaged and in stores a mere 39 days after George Martin first turned on the recording console.

The album is basically a vibrant recitation of their well-honed live act, with a few notable exceptions. Most of it was first-take live recording

34

in the studios; it's the only Beatles album that did not require lots of overdubs.

George Martin, a relative newcomer to the art of recording a pop act, acquits himself well here. His most important contribution to the Beatles debut album was successfully capturing the exuberance and raw energy of these four insouciant Liverpudlians, none of whom was older than 22 at the time of its recording.

Because it was basically recorded on two tracks, the mix is not terribly innovative. The use of reverb and echo to fill out the vocals, especially, is omnipresent throughout the album. The vocals ring with a sonic clarity that totally complements the songs, especially the original compositions.

John Lennon was suffering from a terrible head cold during the recording of this album. This is most notable on two songs—"Anna" and "Baby It's You." You can hear the congestion in his head.

That said, Lennon rips through the covers with wild abandon, giving them a sexy and sassy reading. He treats the originals with a raw reverence that seems to indicate that he knew precisely where the Beatles were headed. And, his guitar playing is vital, if understated.

Paul McCartney's main contribution to this album is his inventive bass playing (typically, for the time, buried in the mixes, with one very notable exception). This is the only Beatles album on which McCartney plays the bass and no other instruments. In time, as we will see, he would turn into a one-man band within the band. McCartney also by now was a dab hand at singing the high harmony that gave the Beatles their signature vocal sound.

George Harrison's guitar playing is tasteful and restrained, for the most part. Like most of his early lead guitar work, his solos tend to fall apart at times. Still, one cannot imagine any other solo being more fitting on all the songs that include a guitar break here.

Ringo Starr does a workmanlike job on the drums, although it's studio musician Andy White who plays on "Love Me Do." Martin wasn't sure that Starr had the musical chops to propel that song along, so he reduced Starr to shaking a tambourine on the track. One other note about his drumming on this album: He hadn't yet gotten into the practice of riding the cymbals so incessantly as to create an obnoxious sibilance in the mix. That was soon to come.

"I Saw Her Standing There": The urgent cry "one, two, three, fah" ushers in one of the Beatles' best rockers ever, and the significance of counting in on their recording career cannot be ignored. They were announcing their arrival on the music scene and world stage in no uncertain terms. "I Saw Her Standing There" is the prototypical Beatles song: Bouncy, catchy, and filled with hooks. That Lennon let a McCartney tune be the opening track on their first album indicates that Lennon—the undisputed leader of the group at this juncture—believed this song was an important representation of the Beatles sound. He was right. McCartney, four months shy of his 22nd birthday, sounds like an experienced adult with randy hankerings. The crackling guitar and the handclaps throughout pump the tune along. This is by far the best bass sound Martin elicited in a mix until the recording of *Rubber Soul* two years later. The screams by McCartney and Lennon before the guitar solo are among the best on any early Beatles recording. The bass, hand claps, drums and lead guitar appear in the left channel, while the lead and harmony vocals and a second guitar appear on the right. And although Lennon's harmonies on the bridge are very effective, they are not spot on. He gets off a note too soon on one occasion, and seems to flub the words on another. This is the best first song on any debut album in rock and roll history.

"Misery": The reverb on this tune is over the top. The vocals, electric guitar, acoustic guitar, piano, and lead and harmony vocals are all the way right, while the drums, bass and lead guitar are on the left. The piano is played by George Martin and only appears during the two bridges. At this point, Martin didn't trust the Beatles' competence on instruments other than their own, so he stepped in here. This would not be the last time he would play an instrument on a Beatles song. The piano is so soaked with reverb that it leeches into the left channel. Listen to Lennon slur the word "send" at the 1:22 mark. Interesting choice. His vocal histrionics at the fade-out are the highlight of this song.

"Anna": One of the best covers ever interpreted by the Beatles, "Anna" is a forlorn tune written by one of Lennon's heroes, the relatively unknown Arthur Alexander. Lennon sings it like he wishes he had written it. The head cold mentioned previously is easily detectable in Lennon's lead vocal, but he somehow turns it into an asset. All the instruments appear on the left and all the vocals appear on the right. Lennon's lead vocal is awash in reverb and echoes eerily in the left channel. Harrison's back-up harmony with McCartney cuts out before McCartney's at 1:00.

"Chains": Harrison's take on the Gerry Goffin–Carole King Brill Building confection. It's a showcase for the three-part harmonies for which the Beatles would forever be known. Vocals all the way right (again) and two guitars, bass and drums all the way left. The wailing harmonica appears on the right, but only during the intro. It sounds like Harrison says "yow" right before the second bridge (at 1:28). A bland and insubstantial song whose entire existence on the album is owed to Lennon and McCartney's charitable habit of giving Harrison and Starr one track on each early album.

"Boys": This is Starr doing his thing, singing from the slightly ponderous point of view of a lovesick teenage girl. Guitars and bass appear on the left, while the drums and vocals appear on the right. Starr's vocal is wet with reverb and bounces around the left channel. Lennon and McCartney amuse themselves with periodic Beatle-like shrieks, and Starr introduces the guitar solo with a encouraging "all right, George!" The solo seems made up on the spot, which is not surprising, considering the thousands of times they must have played this song at the Cavern Club.

"Ask Me Why": An odd and slight departure, with a complicated structure in direct opposition to the straightforward rock conventions on the rest of the album. It's rife with stops and starts, and includes some jazzy guitar chords, including some augmented chords (which were not used often in early pop music). The use of the word "misery" harkens back to the album's second track. Here, the drums, guitars and bass are all on the left channel, with the nonpareil lead and harmony vocals appearing on the right. John's heavily reverbed vocal cracks on the word "cry" 31 seconds into the song. The song ends with the use of a major seventh chord, a musical cliche in jazz standards, but rarely used in pop music up until this point.

"Please Please Me": The best part of the Beatles' first hit record is by far the feel-good lead and harmony vocals. The "come on" back and forth between the lead singer (Lennon) and the backing vocalists (Harrison and McCartney) propel this song to a cascading crescendo that culminates with the hooky title phrase. All of the instruments except the trademark harmonica are to the left, with the vocals all the way right. This is the Merseybeat sound morphing suddenly into radio-ready pop craft of the finest order. The stops-and-starts, punctuated by a simple but effective guitar figure, move this song along at a rapid pace. The middle eight has Harrison as the prominent voice, backed ably by McCartney. The first vocal flub appears at just 14 seconds in, when Lennon and McCartney sing different words, but neither Martin nor the band were inclined to risk tainting such a perfect take by trying to fix a minor glitch. The drums seep into the right channel briefly at the 40-second mark. The second mistake occurs at 1:27. Lennon's slight guffaw on the next "come on" betrays his acknowledgement of the error. Even with two audible mistakes, this is as close to perfect as an early pop song has ever come, and likely ever will.

"Love Me Do": Nice jangling acoustic guitar deep in the mix provides the forward motion in this simple but catchy tune. This is the only song on the album without electric guitars. Since this is a mono tune, no left-right ear candy exists here. Lots of reverb on the word "please." There is a lot of "pleasing" and "misery" on this album.

McCartney had to sing lead at the last minute, when it was discovered that Lennon's mouth would be too busy blowing into the harmonica.

"P.S. I Love You": The sequencing is interesting in that they placed four Lennon-McCartney tunes in a row on an album that only includes eight original compositions. This is the first in a long succession of McCartney tunes that fused pop balladry with rock and roll conventions (such as the vocal exhortations after each line in the last bridge). He even tried out his nascent Elvis voice for the first time on record. The nice cold ending is effective. Another mono recording with almost every sound positioned at just left of center.

"Baby It's You": The impassioned vocal by Lennon turns a nondescript girl group song into a heart-rending cry of anguish by a spurned lover. There is very heavy reverb on both the lead and backing vocals, which gives the vocal track a huge sound. The electric guitar, bass and drums are all the way left, with the vocals and Lennon's acoustic guitar (faint though it may be) on the right. George Martin played the celeste solo, in unison with a bassy electric guitar. Lennon's tortured pleas at the fade-out underscore the heartbreak inherent in the lyrics.

"Do You Want to Know a Secret": A catchy little ditty that suffers from some overly simplistic lyrics and a generally insipid lead vocal by Harrison. It's a Lennon-McCartney composition, but neither of them was inclined to sing such a lightweight song. The electric guitar, drums and bass (which is almost non-existent in the mix) are all the way left, with the vocals and Lennon's acoustic guitar on the right. During the middle eight only, you can hear someone slapping two drumsticks together; since Starr was busy on the drums, it seems likely that Lennon or McCartney provided the extra percussion, or, less likely, either Martin or one of his studio assistants.

"A Taste of Honey": Another cover from their Cavern days, with McCartney's lead vocal as wet as it can be. It sounds like it was recorded in some sort of cavernous environment. The strident repeating of the song's title by Harrison and Lennon gives the song an almost comic feel, as if they were sending up their own schmaltz. A loud electric guitar accompanies the drums and bass on the left channel, while the vocals and another electric guitar are placed at the right. The most interesting parts of this song are the two bridges, where the tempo speeds up, only to slow down again to a syncopated, waltzy pace.

"There's a Place": This song features the same exact start as "Please Please Me": A downbeat, followed by a guitar-harmonica intro. They had to know that this formula couldn't be used for long. They employed a slightly different mix here: Electric guitar, drums, bass and harmonica to the left, and vocals and another electric guitar on the right. When they repeat the song's title during the fade-out the reverb is ramped up, giving it an even bigger overall sound. This is the earliest instance of McCartney's high vocal register totally transforming the backing vocal track.

"Twist and Shout": Recorded at the end of a long day, this Isley Brothers tune was quickly appropriated by the Beatles as one of the most energetic songs in early 1960s pop music. That it has been used in other entertainment media down through the years demonstrates its place as a rock and roll standard. The vocals are all on the right, and the drum track (which can be heard most predominately in the left channel), seems to stray into the right channel at times. Two electric guitars and the bass are also on the left. This is one of Lennon's best-ever vocals: sensual, urgent and appropriately raspy. The ebullient ending, in which Paul yells "yeah" (probably partly in relief after a long, long day in the studio) and Lennon makes a guttural, choking sound, places a huge exclamation point on the completion of their debut album.

With the Beatles

Released November 22, 1963

> "The first set of tricks on the records was double-tracking on the second album. We discovered that, or it was told to us, 'You can do this,' and that really set the ball rolling. We double-tracked ourselves off the album."
>
> *—John Lennon* [3]

> "They just blossomed like an orchid in a hothouse. ... Once they had their first success, they realized they had a way of writing songs that would appeal to the public, and I would say, 'That's marvelous, that's great. Go on and do another one like that, or better, or different, give me something more.'"
>
> *—George Martin* [4]

The Beatles' second album was released on the day that President John F. Kennedy was assassinated. A certain macabre symmetry informs this fact; both JFK and the Beatles are forever associated with the 1960s, and each was a social/cultural figure of astounding breadth and impact.

The second album eventually displaced *Please Please Me* on the pop charts, giving the Beatles full reign over the charts for nearly an entire year. If the Beatles had been unsure of their popularity after the first album, they had to know by now that they were much more than a passing fad, such was their grip on pop fans on both sides of the Atlantic.

George Martin followed the same general formula he had used on the first album, with one subtle but important difference: Throughout *With the Beatles,* the instruments are mixed much louder than the vocals, in some cases overwhelming the singers.

Unlike on the debut album, this time the band used overdubs on several tunes. Also, band members started to branch out by playing instruments other than the ones generally associated with them. This was the first sign that they were becoming more comfortable in the studio, and also presaged the fact that they would never stop looking for new ways to perform old tricks.

Although the 14-song album includes six covers (they were still a couple of albums away from completely exhausting their old stage repertoire), it begins with a three-song gut punch of epic proportions: "It Won't Be Long," "All I've Got to Do" and "All My Loving" were intelligent pop songs, bursting with musical invention and vocal innovation. Anyone dropping the needle on this album would have found it nearly impossible not to listen to the rest of the album after that opening salvo.

All three of those songs also had something else in common: The first sound you hear is the singer's voice (on "All I've Got to Do" there is one guitar chord before the singer's voice, but the full band doesn't come in until the singer makes his appearance). This was a subtle way for the Beatles to admit that what they had to say in their songs now eclipsed the banality of conventional pop music lyrics, as we had known them up to this point.

Tellingly, the first five tracks on the album are original compositions. The covers and the three other originals act essentially as album filler. This is the first sign that the Beatles themselves were comfortable in their craft; their songs were coming out of the same creative mother lode that their rock and roll forebears had mined.

It's also important to note that other than the first three songs, none of the originals stand out as great compositions. This album is padded with covers and weak originals, but is an important development in the Beatles overall sound, and poured fuel on the public conflagration that was Beatlemania.

John Lennon is firmly in control of the band at this point. He sings the first two songs on the album, and his presence is significant on all the songs sung by his bandmates. His singing is top-notch throughout and his rhythm guitar playing drives the band in a way it hadn't on the first album. Even his choice of covers reveals his taste; here he favors Motown and R&B classics that the band had cherished for years.

Paul McCartney has less lead singing to do on this album than he ever did, before or since. He was the chief vocalist on only two original compositions, and one of those is among the weakest songs on the album. His bass playing is economical and pithy, as always, but it's once again buried way too deeply in the mix to have much sonic impact.

McCartney does play a key role as a backing vocalist and harmony partner for Lennon. His vocals shine throughout.

George Harrison contributes his first original composition to a Beatles album, the overly dour "Don't Bother Me." The album fairly rings with Harrison's guitar parts, both lead and rhythm. He also gets to sing a cover song, but unfortunately can barely keep up with the demanding lyrics.

Ringo Starr used this album to once and for all wash away any doubts that George Martin had about Starr's drumming prowess. In fact, the drums get a heavier treatment in the mixes throughout.

"It Won't Be Long": The Beatles' obvious fondness for the word "yeah" is most pronounced on this up-tempo album opener. The call-and-response between Lennon and McCartney and Harrison gives this song a marvelous urgent quality, especially during the bridges, where the backing vocalists are actually telling a backstory under the lead singer's main narrative. The instruments are all the way left (listen for the guitar flub at 46 seconds), with the drums and vocals all the way right. Lennon's lead vocal is double-tracked. Each of the three singers get off the note sung on the last "you" at slightly different times, providing an interesting effect.

"All I've Got to Do": Listen to the band play in perfect communion on this, the second best song on the album. That their well-honed musical chops, polished to near-perfection on stages in Germany and England, could translate so seamlessly to the studio is a tribute to George Martin, but also to the group's clear-eyed devotion to their unique sound. Lennon's lead vocal here oozes with lust, and the choppy guitar part gives the backing track a certain kinkiness. McCartney's high harmonies elevate Lennon's longing vocal to new heights. By now employing a certain tried-and-true mix formula, all the instruments are on the left and the vocals are on the right. You can hear part of the drum track on the right. Check out the brilliant "hmms" during the fade-out; McCartney even hums in harmony.

"All My Loving": "All My Loving" is one of the most perfect pop songs ever written and recorded. It includes the strongest melody on the album, and the playing and singing are flawless. The frenetic pace of the backing track stands in stark contrast to the mournful lyrics about a man missing his lover. McCartney's developing penchant for writing radio-ready pop songs two-plus minutes in duration was showing its face here. Again, all instruments are to the left and the vocals to the right. Harrison's superb guitar solo takes a page out of the James Burton songbook, and Lennon's triple-time strumming on his electric guitar helps to send this song careening to a resounding cold finish in just 2:07. McCartney's lead vocal is double-tracked (a technique he wasn't as fond of as Lennon was), and he even sings the harmony vocal during the final verse, probably because it was beyond the vocal range of Lennon and Harrison. To fully realize how beautiful the melody is, play the song on the piano very slowly, as if it was a ballad. The melody is as haunting and memorable as any Beatles' song, and only the pop dictates of the day—chiefly, that a song needed to be up-tempo to become a hit—obscures the sheer beauty of its melody.

"Don't Bother Me": Harrison's first original composition on a Beatles album is a slight and vaguely whiny tune. This song has no backing vocals, just a double-tracked lead vocal. Because at the time, lead vocal double-tracking required a whole different take in which the singer had to duplicate the original, there are inherent flaws in most double-tracked vocals. Harrison has a particularly rough time with it on this tune; the two vocals he delivered often fall out of synch here, which makes listening to the song slightly off-putting. All the instruments are to the left, as usual, with Starr riding the cymbals throughout the song, but he also added some claves for percussive flavoring. Only on the last phrase of the song does George harmonize with himself.

"Little Child": Seemingly one of the throwaway tracks on this set, "Little Child" has by far the album's most interesting mix to listen to on headphones. The vocals—including the harmonies—are all sung by Lennon and appear in the right channel. McCartney plays a bouncy piano plus bass, and the harmonica, guitars and drums all appear on the left of the stereo spectrum. The only exception to this is during the instrumental break, when Martin switches the harmonica and drums to the right channel temporarily. Someone utters a monosyllabic but unintelligible word 31 seconds into the song. During the two bridges, the "come ons" are doubled by Lennon, but appear on the left channel. This represents significant straying from the usual mix strategy, and portends other deviations in the albums to come.

"Till There Was You": McCartney, at his well-scrubbed choirboy

43

best. His clear Irish tenor nails this show tune, although one wonders if Lennon and Harrison were scratching their heads, trying to figure out what this song had to do with rock and roll. It's a straightforward reading, with McCartney's vocal on the right, and two guitars, bass and claves on the left. It's been written many times that both Harrison and Lennon play nylon-string guitars on this song, but it's not true; only Harrison plays a nylon-string guitar. A close listen on headphones reveals that Lennon is playing a steel-string acoustic.

"Please Mr. Postman": It's true that the Beatles often transformed other people's songs in ways that brought them to a higher musical peak, but this isn't one of those. This is a straightforward treatment of a rather nondescript tune, but one that was featured in some of the band's early live shows. The double-tracked lead vocal by Lennon is solid, and McCartney and Harrison ably back him up. This marks the beginning of Starr's habit of riding the cymbals to annoying effect.

"Roll Over Beethoven": On this Chuck Berry classic, Harrison and Lennon swap roles. On stage in Germany and England, Lennon would sing the lead and Harrison would play the guitar solos. The vocals and handclaps are all the way right, with the instruments on the left. The only deviation from this is two measures of the drum track appearing on the right as soon as Harrison begins singing. Plus, the guitar solo in the middle of the song appears on the right, but not before a one-note premature entry occurs at the 1:27 mark. Harrison has trouble keeping up with the lyrics on the second vocal track that they dubbed over the original. This is also one of those times when Martin concocted a faux ending through the magic of studio editing.

"Hold Me Tight": This song was recorded during the *Please Please Me* sessions, but wound up on the cutting room floor, as it were. That's probably where it should have remained; it's as bland and uninteresting as any Lennon-McCartney tune ever written. Vocals and handclaps (they sure were fond of handclaps as a percussive device on this album) are all the way right, with the drab instrumental track appearing on the left. At two seconds in, and again at 1:11, McCartney sings the word "now," while his back-up singers sing "so." It's interesting that they blew this twice in exactly the same way. At 1:54 you can hear Paul say "um." The song slows down noticeably during the final verse.

"You Really Got a Hold on Me": Without taking anything away

from the sheer brilliance of "Twist and Shout" and "Money"—two of the Beatles' best covers—"You Really Got a Hold on Me" is by far their best cover tune, if only because Lennon dared to cover Smokey Robinson and somehow trumped his version. The blue-eyed soul of Lennon's vocal performance here elevates this song to new heights. All of the instruments are to the left, except for the piano, played by George Martin. The piano reverts to the left channel during the rest of the song. Lennon harmonizes with himself on the verses, before McCartney and Harrison join him during the choruses. Unlike many tunes sung by Lennon, this one is not soaked with reverb, and as a result, the vocal is drier and clearer. The most curious aspect of this recording is the elimination of four measures of the drum track appearing in the right channel 25 seconds into the song. When the catalogue was remastered in 2009, this anomaly was corrected. There are other instances of corrections made during the 2009 remastering (we'll examine this further when we deconstruct "Day Tripper").

"I Wanna Be Your Man": Lennon and McCartney gave this throw-away tune to Starr to sing, but they also gave it to a little known up-and-coming band called the Rolling Stones, who turned it into their first hit. The track features all the instruments—including an organ played with demonic delight by Lennon—on the left channel, except during the instrumental break, when Martin pans the instruments over slightly to the right. There is a lot going on deep in the background on this track. At 45 seconds, McCartney utters the word "hip," and someone utters an unintelligible few words at 1:14. McCartney says "ooh" at 1:29. Listen for the handclaps deep in the mix on the right during the last verse only.

"Devil in Her Heart": This is a cover of a recording by a Detroit group called the Donays, who recorded it as "Devil in His Heart." Harrison takes the lead vocal here. A strange thing happens on this track. The backing singers—Lennon and McCartney—sing the first line before the lead vocalist comes in. When Harrison sings his first line, it's clearly an edited, punched in take. Listen from 11 seconds to 14 seconds in and you'll be able to hear the punched in edit. All other sound, except for Harrison's voice, is missing on just this one line in the right channel. Martin turns up the electric guitar in the mix during the outro. This track also features a much bigger and imposing drum sound than most of the other songs on this album.

"Not a Second Time": This is the first in a long litany of Lennon songs dealing with the subjects of trust and jealousy. George Martin plays the darkly ominous piano part, and the instrumental break—which comes in after only one verse—is essentially a piano solo playing the song's melody. Lennon says "yeah" at 1:01. This is really a quirky song, filled with strange chords and odd twists and turns. Lennon double-tracks his vocal during the fade-out.

"Money": The song starts out with the piano playing the recurrent riff, and just four taps by Starr on his hi hat, before the full band bursts in. This is one of the most interesting mixes on the album. George Martin's piano is the only thing in the right channel, with the other instruments all to the left. But all the vocals appear just left of center in the stereo spectrum. This time, they limited the hand claps to the instrumental break. McCartney creates some vocal histrionics on the rather lengthy fade-out.

A Hard Day's Night

RELEASED JULY 10, 1964

> "With the great advance of four-track we were able to overdub and put on secondary voices and guitar solos afterwards. By the time we did *A Hard Day's Night* we would certainly put the basic track down and do the vocals afterwards. Invariably, I was putting all the rhythm instruments onto either one or two tracks so you would have bass lumped with guitar. It wasn't until later still that we began putting bass on afterwards as well, giving Paul the opportunity of using his voice more."
>
> *—George Martin*[5]

A Hard Day's Night marks a watershed moment in Beatle history. It is one of their best albums, and the only one to date that contained only songs written by Lennon and McCartney. There are no cover tunes, and there isn't even a token song sung by their loveable drummer (a fact that would be rectified on most of their future albums).

By now, of course, the band had been introduced to mainstream America via their appearances on the *Ed Sullivan Show* in February of 1964, as well as the almost omnipresent airplay they received on the radio. Now, there were starring in their first feature film on the big screen, named after the title song on this album. The Beatles chose the first seven tracks on the album as the songs most worthy for inclusion in the film, but the six tracks that follow would have been just as worthy.

This publicity barrage (in combination with their constant touring schedule) might have been enough to make any lesser act at least mildly interesting to the masses, but the Beatles had a secret weapon: undeniably catchy songs, sung and played with a brio borne of their youth and enthusiasm, and emboldened by their conquer-the-world mentality.

A Hard Day's Night contains 13 masterfully constructed pop songs with hummable melodies that seemed to linger in the listener's head even after just one listen. It's important to recall the state of pop music in 1964: Most groups (and individual artists, for that matter) built their album strategy on a simple calculus: Take a surefire hit, put it on an album padded with 11 throwaway songs, and watch the teenyboppers buy it in droves. The Beatles never believed in this strategy; they were all about quality control, making sure their writing, singing and playing matched their high ideals and rewarded their fans with a sterling product.

While their first two albums established a formula and a unique sound, *A Hard Day's Night* upped the ante considerably by dint of the blue ribbon songwriting partnership that John Lennon and Paul McCartney had forged. Prior to the album's release, other artists—completely aware of the Beatles' popularity—hoped that the band would cover their tunes, thereby giving their songs a second shelf life in the pop charts. Now, other artists were clamoring for Lennon and McCartney to *write* them a song. The weakest song on *A Hard Day's Night* could have been a hit for just about anyone else; such was the power of the almost peerless song-craft Lennon and McCartney had tapped into.

The album is also very interesting to listen to on headphones, if only for the simple fact that it's their first album recorded entirely on four-track. Now, George Martin had more options when deciding where to place each vocal and instrument in the stereo spectrum.

Make no mistake about it, John Lennon dominates this album in a way he never would again. The first three tracks are his, and nine of the 13 tracks are dominated by his vocals. Five of the last six songs on the album feature Lennon as lead vocalist, and there isn't a weak one in the group. Lennon also started to use his 12-string electric guitar more frequently here, making the rhythm guitar parts ring with a newfound clarity.

Paul McCartney's three songs on *A Hard Day's Night* were of such high quality that they would have provided a nice career for anyone else. McCartney makes his first foray into original balladry, and he rocks out on his other two tunes. Even the volume of his bass begins to creep up in the mix, at least on some of the tunes. As always, he's the perfect harmony vocal foil for Lennon; their voices mesh in new and inventive ways on this album.

Harrison gets to sing a Lennon-McCartney original (perhaps the weakest song on the set), but it's his guitar that makes him one of the stars of the show. From the 12-string electric he plays on the title tune, to the nylon-string acoustic that gives "And I Love Her" its signature sound, Harrison's work throughout is as tasty as it gets.

Although Starr doesn't get to sing, he bashes his kit with wild abandon, backing the band with his idiosyncratic but tasteful style.

"A Hard Day's Night": The title track officially ushers in Beatlemania, if only because we associate it with the scene in the film where the boys are running to escape from their fans. On its own, it's a tremendous musical achievement: Urgent, frenetic and filled with buoyant vocals and guitars. From the first startling chord, to the chiming 12-string electric guitar that plays it out, it's 2:33 of the finest rock and roll in the twentieth century. Two electric guitars, bass and drums are all the way left, and on the right we find a cowbell played by McCartney, plus some out of control bongos getting smacked by Starr. The electric guitar solo is doubled note for note by George Martin's piano, resulting in an earthy sound. Lennon's double-tracked vocal handles the verses, while McCartney's double-tracked vocals handle the bridges (possibly because they were out of Lennon's vocal range). In any case, it's fitting that an album comprised of some of the best songs the two had ever written features an opening track on which they share the lead vocal duties.

"I Should Have Known Better": This is a refreshing example of the new mix options at Martin's disposal brought about by the introduction of four-track recording. Lennon's lead vocal is centered, then doubled and placed to the right in the stereo picture, giving the vocals a bigger, more dominating sound. One vocal is centered during the bridges, but when Lennon goes high, they double it again. The acoustic guitar, drums and bass (which you can hardly hear) are to the left, and the electric guitar and the 12-string electric guitar solo—both played by Harrison—are on the right.

"If I Fell": A beautiful love song deftly handled with perfect harmonies by Lennon and McCartney. Lennon's lead vocal is double-tracked, but McCartney's is a single voice. The vocals are centered. Listen for McCartney's stumble on the word "vain" at 1:45. The acoustic guitar, drums and bass are way over left, and the electric guitar is panned right, *except* when it makes its brief appearance between the first and second verse. For three seconds, it appears in the middle of the mix, then returns to the right for the rest of the song. Two important mixing observations should be made at this point: First, Martin is getting a pretty meaty sound out of the acoustic guitars on this album, something that was missing on the first two albums. Second, except for one or two instances, this album is notable for its almost total lack of reverb, echo and other sound-sweetening devices. Most of the vocals are completely dry.

"I'm Happy Just to Dance with You": Simple mix here: Drums and bass on the left, and two electric guitars on the right. The only anomaly is the bass drum that appears just right of center only during the verses. This is the weakest track on the album, and seems like it was dashed off hurriedly to give Harrison a song to sing. Lennon and McCartney's backing "ohs" have been treated with some reverb, which gives them a big sound that at times threatens to overwhelm Harrison's lead vocal. This was the second and final time that Lennon and McCartney wrote a song for Harrison to sing.

"And I Love Her": A remarkable tune because of its simple elegance and dramatic but understated instrumental track. McCartney's vocal is double-tracked and centered in the mix. Just under his vocal, you can hear the tapping of some wood blocks, which also veers slightly into the right channel. The driving acoustic guitar played by Lennon keeps the band tight, and bass and percussion are all the way left. Harrison's beautifully played nylon string guitar introduces each verse, and lays down a nice counterpoint during the times he plays the Latin-tinged riff under McCartney's vocal. The idea to modulate into a higher key for the guitar solo gives the song some added drama. It also was a master stroke to end a song played essentially in a minor key on its relative major chord. Listen for McCartney to hum the first few notes of Harrison's guitar figure on the outro.

"Tell Me Why": The effect of recording three voices and four instruments, all in a semi-live take gives this song a Wall of Sound-type of vibe. It's incredibly simple, with bass and drums on the left, and piano and electric guitar on the right (although the electric guitar does sneak over to the middle occasionally). Although all the vocals are centered, during the middle eight Lennon's vocal is panned to the right. His vocals are double-tracked and he sings the wrong words on one of the vocals at 1:01. Listen for the odd squeaking sound all the way left at 2:05.

"Can't Buy Me Love": This song has a couple features that are particular to the Beatles' sound. First, it includes one of the best guitar solos in any Beatles song. It also features one of the best screams on record, this time courtesy of McCartney.

His double-tracked vocals are sung with an uncommon bravado, making his inability to synch the two vocals on the final "oh" a minor nitpick. The drums, bass and acoustic guitar are all the way left, with the acoustic being much more prominent in the intro before Martin pots it down for the rest of the song. The electric guitar is on the right, except for the solo, which is on two guitars, one of which is centered. This anomaly occurred as a result of Harrison recording the original solo, with the band later deciding to wipe the original solo and re-record it. Faint remnants of the original solo account for it sounding like two guitars. They do not play the same solo; there are subtle differences in the two parts. (This same phenomena can be heard on the guitar solo on "I'm Down.") Listen for McCartney's exuberant "hey" toward the end of the solo at 1:27.

"Anytime at All": There is a very interesting mix on this tune. Lennon sings the first line, and McCartney the second, with both of them doubled. Their vocals are split so that they appear at just left of center, and just right of center in the stereo picture. Electric guitar, drums, bass and acoustic guitar are all the way left, with the drums meandering slightly into the right channel. There is also a piano on the right, playing simple bass notes rather than full chords. The electric guitar solo also appears on the right. This is another example of a song that has a heavily edited ending in which most of the instruments are eliminated, with just the drums, bass and a single guitar playing the final chord.

"I'll Cry Instead": A simple song, with a double-tracked Lennon lead vocal that appears at center and to the right. An acoustic guitar and

50

tambourine are heard in the right channel. The electric guitar, drums and a bass part that is uncharacteristically prominent in the mix can be heard all the way left.

"Things We Said Today": From the first slamming triplet on the acoustic guitar (it's an A minor chord), this song chugs along with a stridency that is appealing. It veers from a minor key during the verses to a major key during the bridges, without losing any of its dramatic feel. Another acoustic guitar, as well as electric guitar, bass and drums are panned left, while a tambourine and piano are all the way right, but only during the bridges. McCartney's vocal is doubled by a low harmony part that he sings under the lead vocal. Listen for his vocal trip on the word "on" at 1:27. Single hits on the tambourine can be heard all the way right on the outro fade.

"When I Get Home": The dissonant vocal intro is sung by the lead singer (Lennon), and the backing singer (McCartney), and appears all the way right. When Lennon sings the verse, his vocal is centered. The drums, bass and electric guitar are all the way left. A second electric guitar is in the center, but leaks into the right channel ever so slightly. An odd song that seems to be about a man looking forward to returning to his lover/wife, but then turns into the story of a man fearful of having his romantic tryst discovered. Weird phrases and words abound; cows are coming home and trivialities galore!

"You Can't Do That": Another one of Lennon's jealousy songs, played in a raucous style replete with cowbell and a 12-string electric guitar solo played by Lennon. As usual on this album, the drums, bass and electric guitar are panned all the way left (except for the solo, which appears in the right channel). Lennon's lead vocal, the backing vocals and the cowbell are all centered in the mix. Listen for the odd ending, where the electric guitar and bass slowly come to a stop together. This technique was cribbed by Three Dog Night several years later on their hit song "Mama Told Me Not to Come."

"I'll Be Back": A simple but beautifully rendered acoustic ballad, with nifty harmonies and, as in "Things We Said Today," a recurring minor to major key shift. Contrary to popular belief, there are actually three acoustic guitars on this tune, one each in the left, center and right of the stereo picture. Lennon's lead vocal is doubled, although they are not in synch briefly at :45 into the song.

Beatles for Sale

RELEASED DECEMBER 4, 1964

"Our records were progressing. We'd started out like anyone spending their first time in a studio—nervous and naïve and looking for success. By this time, we'd had loads of hits and a few tours and were becoming more relaxed with ourselves, and more comfortable in the studio. And the music was getting better."

—George Harrison [6]

"Some of the material on *Beatles for Sale* was just brilliant. What was happening elsewhere was nothing like it."

—Ringo Starr [7]

Beatles for Sale was recorded over a three-week period in the fall of 1964, during the Beatles' most arduous year. While not a bad album at all, it serves as sort of a placeholder for the band as they perfected their live chops at the expense of extended time in the recording studio. It's the weakest album of their first four, although it does have two seriously good songs on it.

The songs are superbly played and sung; it's clear that the Beatles were really a finely honed little rock and roll outfit by this time. In terms of mixes, it's pretty straightforward. Almost every track has the bass, drums and an acoustic guitar on the left channel, and electric guitars and the very occasional piano on the right channel. Most of the vocals are centered in the mix, with a few notable exceptions.

The release of *Beatles for Sale* came just five months after *A Hard Day's Night* was unleashed on the masses. More than anything, this demonstrates the zeal of the record company to get more Beatles product on the market as soon as possible in order to capitalize on their overwhelming popularity. Today, of course, that strategy would never work. It takes nearly five months for today's artists to record one song, let alone two albums. To release two full albums in a five-month span today would risk overexposing the artist and alienating his or her fans. That was obviously not a concern regarding Beatles fans in that heady year of 1964. Most importantly, the Beatles somehow kept the quality of their product at peak levels.

Once again, it's John Lennon who rules the roost on this album. He's the lead singer on the first four tracks, and his vocal prominence can be felt on nine of the album's 14 songs. Also, his distinctive acoustic guitar can be heard on nine tracks here, as the album has a decidedly country-rock bent to it.

Paul McCartney is the lead singer on just three of the 14 tracks. However, once again he adds perfect flavor to most of the tracks with his sublime harmony vocals and his bass-playing prowess, which grew to new levels on each album and took a significant leap forward on this one.

George Harrison's voice can't really be heard until he takes a turn on one of his beloved covers tunes on the album's final track. However, Harrison's signature electric guitar sound really coalesced on this album; it's full of twangy, jangly tones that pay tribute to Carl Perkins and James Burton, among other guitar heroes of his.

Ringo Starr does workmanlike duty on the drums throughout. Never overwhelming any one song and, as usual, complementing all of them in an understated but rock steady manner.

"No Reply": The first thing you hear on *Beatles for Sale* is John Lennon's incomparable voice. Here he builds on themes of jealousy that would be woven in and out of his original material throughout his career, both with the Beatles and during his solo career. As on most of the songs on this album, the acoustic guitar, drums and bass are over to the left, and the lead vocal is centered. Lennon harmonizes with himself in certain spots, and McCartney's high harmony is added for dramatic counterpoint. Listen for a mumbled single word at the 15-second mark. On the right you can hear a piano in spots, but most predominately during the middle eight. Also, a crash cymbal appears on the right at just the time you expect it to. Listen for the subtle finger snaps on the last verse only.

"I'm a Loser": Who thinks to write a song called "I'm a Loser?" John Lennon does. He was slowly morphing from loveable moptop to introspective singer/songwriter, right before our eyes. This song is a marvel of self-effacement and self-questioning. Slowly weaning themselves from a musical device that was previously found on many of their songs, "I'm a Loser" is the only song on this album to feature a harmonica. One can imagine Lennon tipping his hat to Bob Dylan on the most Dylan-like song in the Beatles catalogue (up to this point in time). An acoustic guitar, a buried bass guitar, a very muted electric guitar and the drums are all the way left, with the lead guitar and a tambourine (played only during the choruses) are on the right. Listen for Harrison's guitar flub on the solo during the outro.

"Baby's in Black": Here, Lennon and McCartney explore how colors can affect or explain moods, just like they were to do in the single B-side, "Yes It Is." The harmonies between Lennon and McCartney on the two-line bridges are spine-tingling and thrilling. Lennon's lead vocal is centered, but a second Lennon vocal is panned slightly to the right to achieve a bigger sound. Acoustic and electric guitars, bass and drums are all the way left, while the lead electric guitar, played only during the bridges and the solo, is all the way right. Listen to Harrison uncharacteristically bend the notes on his guitar on the last verse, when a tambourine makes its first appearance in the mix.

"Rock and Roll Music": A splendid take on a Chuck Berry classic, this remains one of the finest Beatles covers of all-time, if only for the gutbucket lead vocal delivered by Lennon. Listen to him chew off the words "rock and roll" at the beginning of each verse, rendering the phrase slightly differently each time, but always with what could only be called a vocal snarl. He's delivering lyrics so quickly that at one point (1:36), he eschews the connective "and" in the phrase. A fairly simple mix here, with drums and bass on the left, and piano and electric guitar on the right. The piano part inexplicably disappears from 1:45 until 1:52.

"I'll Follow the Sun": Five songs in, we finally get to hear McCartney take over the lead vocal chores (ever so briefly). This song is most notable for its brevity and wistfulness, and also for its use of an acoustic guitar as the main instrument, something McCartney would employ increasingly more often in the years just ahead. The acoustic guitar, bass and a light tapping on a packing crate for percussion are on the left; two electric guitars—one played only during the solo break—are on the right. Listen how Lennon's low harmony vocal seems to overwhelm McCartney's lead vocal on the two bridges.

"Mr. Moonlight": Written by Roy Lee Johnson and first recorded by Dr. Feelgood and the Interns, this song was for a long time part of the Beatles' live act, before they had a significant pool of original material to offer up to live audiences. The recording is a study in hokum, with the Beatles using the novelty tune as a way to release some of the pressure they surely felt to come up with the next hit record. Both Lennon and McCartney totally chew the vocal scenery by over-singing their respective parts, and the Hammond organ McCartney plays throughout has an extra thick layer of cheese on it. Two electric guitars, a bass and the drums can be found all the way on the left. There is also an unidentifiable squeaking sound heard on the left channel throughout the song. Perhaps McCartney's organ stops needed oiling, or maybe it's the sound of George Harrison wheeling in the African-like bass drum he plays for dramatic effect at selected moments and heard on the right channel.

"Kansas City/Hey Hey Hey Hey!": This is the sound of a very polished, in-sync rock and roll band. From the opening guitar flurry to the faded out call-and-response, this tune rocks out with a fervor rivaled by McCartney's vocals on "I'm Down" and "Long Tall Sally." An electric guitar, drums and bass are on the left channel, while the lead electric guitar, piano, a cacophony of backing vocals and during the last two verses only, hands claps, flood the right channel. McCartney's lead vocal really brings it, and his scream preceding the guitar solo is otherworldly. The backing vocals are so over-modulated and so soaked in reverb that they are a little difficult to listen to on headphones.

"Eight Days a Week": A song layered in rich harmonies and interesting innovations, "Eight Days a Week" could have been a single, if the Beatles had chosen to make it one. As it was, the song did chart, an unusual occurrence for non-singles during this era. The song is faded in, a technique not widely used at the time. The acoustic and electric guitar, bass and drums are all the way to the left, while persistent handclaps and the backing harmony vocals are on the right. The handclaps are noticeably louder on the last verse. Lennon's double-tracked lead vocal appears in both the center and the right of the stereo picture. Harrison and McCartney provide the perfect harmonies.

"Words of Love": Lennon and McCartney completely deconstruct and put back together again this Buddy Holly classic, a long-time favorite of both men. The chiming electric guitars courtesy of Lennon and Harrison, both playing the same exact part, give this song the kind of shimmer and elegance that it calls for. The guitars are brought way up in the mix during the instrumental breaks, and are underlain with some very light handclaps. Bass, drums and tambourine are on the left, with one electric guitar centered and the other on the right. Listen to the superb harmony vocals, sung by all three primary Beatles singers, morphing "hmms" into "aahs" during the fade out.

"Honey Don't": This is the first of many forays into country-and-western singing that Ringo Starr would trot out over the years. This time, a simple backing (bass, drums and tambourine on the left; acoustic and electric guitars on the right) ably backs up the singer, who orders up the Harrison-played guitar solos by name. The bass is brought way up in the mix on this track, a refreshing departure from the norm.

"Every Little Thing": This underrated little gem has a lot going on in it. John Lennon plays the inventive electric guitar solo, and provides the double-tracked lead vocal, with harmonies from McCartney. McCartney's harmony goes slightly sharp on the last line during the fade-out. Listen for the tapping of the wooden body of the acoustic during the intro. That guitar, along with bass and drums, appears in the left channel, while the electric guitar, piano and a timpani can be heard on the right. The piano and drums cut out entirely during the fade-out.

"I Don't Want to Spoil the Party": With "I'm a Loser," this is one of the two best songs on the album. Typically for this period, they are chiefly Lennon songs with that familiar undercurrent of jealousy and suspicion intact. Lennon sings the low harmony under his own lead vocal, with McCartney coming in to tackle the high parts during the bridges. Listen for the two rapid succession "woos" right before the electric guitar solo, delivered with aplomb by Harrison. Acoustic guitar and drums are on the left, with the electric guitar and bass on the right. Starr hits his hi hat only during the bridges.

"What You're Doing": The last of McCartney's three solo vocal appearances on this album, with "oohs" and "aahs" provided by Lennon and Harrison. The drums, electric guitar and bass are on the left, with a second lead electric guitar and acoustic guitar on the right. The lead guitar solo gets panned to the center and is paired with a rollicking piano part, played mostly on the bass keys. The timpani is prominent in the intro and fade-out.

"Everybody's Trying to Be My Baby": Harrison gives one more nod toward Carl Perkins before the proceedings end here. The most surprising development on this track is that Harrison's lead vocal (heretofore unheard from on the previous 13 tracks) is awash with reverb and, especially, echo, two effects he had a very well-known aversion to. The drums, bass and acoustic guitar are panned all the way left, but let's face it: This song exists solely to let Harrison exercise his well-executed guitar parts in tribute to his hero, Perkins. The various solos appear on the right channel.

Help!

RELEASED AUGUST 13, 1965

"With everything, with any kind of thing, my aim seems to be to distort it. Distort it from what we know it as, even with music, with visual things. But the aim is to change it from what it is to see what it could be. To see the potential in it all. The point is to take a note and wreck the note and see in that note what else there is in it that a simple act like distorting it has caused. It's the same with film. Take it and superimpose on top of it so you can't quite tell what it is anymore. It's all trying to create magic, it's all trying to make things happen that you don't know why they've happened. I'd like a lot more things to happen like they did when you were kids when you didn't know how the conjuror did it."

—*Paul McCartney* [8]

"The Beatles didn't get totally immersed in record production until later on, when they stopped touring. Until then, they didn't have time. They would dash into the studio and put down their tracks and then leave all the work to us."

—*George Martin* [9]

At the tail end of Beatlemania's apogee, the Beatles were exhausted from a rigorous worldwide touring schedule, and the demands of turning out new singles and albums for the recording company (and the fans).

They spent most of the early part of 1965 traveling to exotic locales (Austria, the Bahamas and many points in between) to film the movie *Help!,* their second feature film and the first to be shot in color. Less autobiographical thematically than *A Hard Day's Night, Help!* traded on the sure-fire formula of showing the lads up to their antic tricks in a campy send-up of the James Bond film franchise. Superb eye candy for teenaged Beatlemaniacs, to be sure, but the puerile and kitschy quality of the film failed to foreshadow the Beatles' growing dissatisfaction with the rigors of their pop star lifestyles.

A world-weariness had set in, and although it hadn't yet completely infected the songs, it was not far around the bend. On their next album, the darkness would slowly begin to emerge, as they verged closer and closer to abandoning touring all together.

Help! is an interesting album, but really in the middle of the pack on any list of their best LPs. There are a couple or three really fine songs, but there's also a lot of filler. Unlike several previous LPs and a couple still to be made, George Martin did not pan all the vocals to one side, and the rhythm track to the other. Most of the lead vocals here are more or less centered in the stereo spectrum.

Also, all four Beatles play on every track, except for two. This would happen less frequently on subsequent recordings. The 14 tunes here add up to 34:21 in elapsed time. This is the final LP in which the Beatles felt compelled to include a couple of covers.

It is one of the least-interesting Beatles albums to listen to on headphones. There is very little in the way of studio tricks or funny little vocal quirks on *Help!* It's as straightforward an album as they ever made. For all its flaws, any album that contains "Ticket to Ride," "You've Got to Hide Your Love Away," "You're Going to Lose That Girl" and "Yesterday" must be considered an unmitigated triumph.

Still in all, the album suffers from an odd sequencing. "Side one" is almost all Lennon, and "side two" has only two Lennon songs, and three in a row sung by McCartney. Moreover, the first seven songs, which are on the *Help!* movie soundtrack, are far superior to the seven tunes they added to pad the album.

This is a Lennon album, for sure. Although he sang lead on just six of the 14 tracks, his songs (and his singing) totally overshadowed those by his mates. Also, his acoustic guitar playing on this album is superb. He drives the rhythm section throughout. He was clearly still leading the group at this juncture.

Strangely, except for "Yesterday" and McCartney's superlative harmonies and backing vocals (and occasional scintillating guitar solos), he does not have an overwhelming presence on this LP. His songs are not up to their usual high standards and his bass is almost completely buried. Crank up the bass on the EQ on the song "Help!" and you can still just barely hear it.

Harrison's guitar sounds great, but his two compositions are as weak as anything he's ever written. Starr's drumming on "Ticket to Ride" is ground-breaking, but other than that, you don't notice him much. On a couple of songs, his part is almost invisible.

"Help!": One of the best Beatles songs ever. Lennon's playing his Guild 12-string, a guitar he used (as far as I can tell) on only two other Beatles songs: "You've Got to Hide Your Love Away" and "The Continuing Story of Bungalow Bill." Starr is playing with the trap off his snare. Harrison's lead guitar is great, although it took him a long time to perfect the part. It's awash with reverb. Drums and bass are all the way left, and the 12-string and electric guitar are on the right. You can faintly hear Lennon tapping on his acoustic during the electric guitar figure that ends each verse.

"The Night Before": Great vocal, soaked with reverb and doubled, a very un–McCartney-like technique. Very interesting backing vocals by Lennon and Harrison. It's Lennon playing the electric piano. Starr is riding the cymbals, of course. A great harmony guitar solo, doubled by Harrison, as they were fond of this technique during this era. Drums and bass are on the left, and an electric piano and electric guitar are on the right. The doubled solo appears in the center.

"You've Got to Hide Your Love Away": Great lyrics and a spine-tingling, sleepy vocal. During the first verse, there's a decided raspiness in Lennon's voice. Here's the 12-string again. On the chorus there is a second guitar, playing pieces of the melody, especially the descending notes that lead into the chorus, all the way right where a tambourine can also be heard. And, there are two flutes on the outro.

"I Need You": Lennon and McCartney sound completely bored on the backing vocals. There is a terribly intrusive cowbell on the bridges. Again, virtually no bass guitar can be heard on this track. They are using the same volume pedal guitar effect they employed on "Yes it Is." Harrison's doubled vocal gets badly out of synch at :36. On the left are the acoustic guitar, drums and bass, with the electric guitar, backing vocals and cowbell on the right.

"Another Girl": Son (or daughter) of "The Night Before." McCartney plays lead, almost perfectly mimicking the guitar figure he used on the outro for "Ticket to Ride." This is of a piece with "She's A Woman," what with its "stabbing" guitar part. The drums and bass are on the left, with an acoustic and two electric guitars on the right. All vocals are centered. This song has a very odd ending, with a brief guitar solo playing the whole thing out.

"You're Going to Lose That Girl": The piano on the opening is almost exactly like that on "Not a Second Time." The congas are spastic and often out of rhythm. Great, simple guitar solo played by Harrison. Listen for the interesting key change at the bridges. Electric guitar, drums and bass are left, while the right channel features the congas, piano and the guitar solo. This tune sounds so happy for a song with such dour lyrics.

"Ticket to Ride": Great lead guitar played by McCartney, and crunchy, chiming guitars throughout. The tambourine comes in one measure too early on the first middle eight at 1:08. Lennon's using the ADT he loved so much. His vocal here is one of the best ever Beatles vocal performances. Great falsetto by Lennon at the outro. The drums, bass and one electric guitar are all the way left, with Lennon's lead vocal (doubled only on the word "ride") and McCartney's high harmony centered. The lead guitar and tambourine are also in the center of the stereo picture, and faint handclaps can be heard on the outro only. The electric guitar played by Lennon is the only thing heard on the right channel. They must have been excited by this song; the recording is inventive, the track is almost flawless and it sounded like nothing else on the radio at the time.

"Act Naturally": Some thought Lennon and/or McCartney sang harmony on this countrified ditty, but listen closely: it's all Starr. Again, the acoustic guitar, drums and bass are all the way left, and the overbearing electric guitar and harmony vocal are panned right, along with Starr's persistent hitting of the rim of his snare drum, which gives the track a tickety-tack sound throughout.

"It's Only Love": Great track with a superb vocal, despite what Lennon apparently thought about it. The chords are so Lennon; he was listening to too many girl groups at this point. He's double-tracked on the chorus, which adds dramatic weight to the song. The second voice is slightly delayed to give the overall vocal performance a beefier sound. The song, played in the key of C, has Lennon's acoustic guitar capoed up to the fifth fret, so he's actually playing the chord progression using the key of G configurations. Two acoustic guitars and the drums are on the left, and the bass apparently is, too, although it's almost impossible to discern. There are two wacky sounding electric guitars on the right, with a tambourine on the choruses only. Listen for the extra dollop of wah-wah on the last note.

"You Like Me Too Much": One of the worst original songs ever recorded by the Beatles. The track is clumsy, the lyrics are abysmal and it just doesn't go anywhere. There are two electric pianos during the intro. Contrary to what you've probably always thought, Harrison is the only singer on this track. The electric piano that plays the intro on the left channel moves over to the right during the course of the song. Bass, drums, acoustic guitar and tambourine are all the way left, while the electric piano and electric guitar (which only appears during the solo interplay with the electric piano), are all on the right channel.

"Tell Me What You See": A song unlike almost anything they ever did, with the faux Latin rhythm and the interesting percussion, including a guiro, one of the only uses of this Spanish percussion instrument ever by the band. Also, conventional drums, woodblocks and a tambourine round out the percussion lineup. Strangely, McCartney sings the harmony on the first and third lines of each verse, but takes the lead vocal on the rest of the song. Lennon sounds mildly disinterested, although the harmonies between he and McCartney are more complex than usual. Harrison does not sing on this tune. An electric piano can be heard on the right channel; they were using electric keyboards much more frequently on *Help!* than on any previous album.

"I've Just Seen a Face": Great 12-string acoustic intro, with McCartney playing his Ovation Balladeer (which he rarely used to record). There is no bass on this song. The second guitar part is interesting. Only McCartney sings on this tune, placing a high harmony under his lead vocal on the choruses. Wouldn't be at all surprised if he recorded this song all on his own, although there is a muted drum sound in the left channel. The 12-string guitar solo, played mostly on the bass strings, is interesting. Maracas can be heard on the right, and just a faint whiff of another acoustic guitar can be heard in the center, under the vocals.

"Yesterday": This song represents a watershed moment in the Beatles' development as songwriters, and also in the dynamic of the group. It's the first time that only one member of the group appeared on one of their songs, and also the first time in which strings (and not a standard rock and roll instrument) provided the predominant accompaniment to the singer. It's surprising, given McCartney's well-documented affection for this song, that he allowed it to be relegated to the second side of the album, which only included songs that did not appear in the film. It could have died a lonely death, but was saved by its undeniably stark majesty, its haunting melody and its incomparable bathos. And also, by it's innovation; no other rock and roll band had yet recorded a song of groundbreaking introspection and instrumentation. It changed the rock and roll landscape forever. It also changed how Lennon and McCartney regarded their writing partnership, and opened up the floodgates to heretofore uncharted waters in terms of how they worked together, or more accurately, how they might put forward their own individual compositions (albeit with the previously agreed upon Lennon-McCartney writing credit intact). "Yesterday" has astoundingly profound lyrics, especially considering that there weren't too many songs like this on the charts at the time. McCartney's vocal leans toward the right in the stereo mix, with the strings almost all the way to the left. He's double-tracked on the bridges. His great acoustic part is played without a pick. He actually plays the bass part with his thumb on his acoustic guitar. At 1:44 you can hear him hit the wood on his guitar inadvertently. When you listen to this song, keep in mind that it's author was 23 years old at the time. This was definitely a game-changer.

"Dizzy Miss Lizzie": The doubled lead guitars played by Lennon and Harrison are scintillating. Lennon's vocal is recorded using ADT, but his vocal is inspired (and wet with reverb, one of the only songs on the entire LP that is swimming in reverb). This song contains a couple of the finest Beatle screams ever committed to tape. The bass and drums are to the left, with both electric guitars on the right, although one of the guitars temporarily leaks into the center of the mix. An electric piano can also be heard in the center of the mix. At this point in their career, it seems odd that they would have the final song on one of their albums be a cover song.

Rubber Soul

RELEASED DECEMBER 3, 1965

"We were really starting to find ourselves in the studio. We were finding what we could do, just being the four of us and playing our instruments.

The overdubbing got better, even though it was always pretty tricky because of the tracks. The songs got more interesting, so with that the effects got more interesting."

—Ringo Starr[10]

"We finally took over the studio. In the early days, we had to take what we were given. We had to make it in two hours or whatever it was. And three takes was enough, and we didn't know about 'you could get more bass,' and we were learning the technique. With *Rubber Soul*, we were more precise about making the album—that's all. We took over the cover and everything."

—John Lennon[11]

Rubber Soul is a monumental musical step forward for the Beatles, and presaged the unrelenting craft and innovation that the following two albums would feature. It's also the first album since *Please Please Me* that the Beatles didn't record piecemeal; that is, whenever they had time away from traveling the world. This is the first time the Beatles recorded an album as a concentrated effort to capture a cohesive sound, unfettered by the pull of having to be someplace else.

The album was recorded in a four-week period during October and November 1965. It was also the first album on which they made more liberal use of the possibilities that a four-track recording machine offered. As a result, the mixes are a little more daring, and much more interesting to listen to on headphones.

For the first time, the Beatles' lyrics were filled with notes of simmering discontent: "You Won't See Me," "Nowhere Man," "I'm Looking Through You" and "Run for Your Life" are all songs imbued with an aura of insecurity, jealousy and galloping distrust. Lennon includes the word "dead" in no less than three of his compositions here (he would opine further on the subject in two songs on the next album). It's dark stuff from those lovable moptops.

The entire 14-song album clocks in at just 35:50, but the run time is filled with incredible musicianship, tasty arrangements, near flawless singing and an urgent sense that the band is reaching new heights heretofore unattained by their counterparts in the business. This is the point at which they pulled away from the rock and roll pack. The album is heavy with acoustic guitars and reflective, folky undertones; there is not a lot of out-and-out rock and roll on *Rubber Soul*. This is not an album to listen to on Saturday night, but it'll make your Sunday afternoon a lot sweeter. The songwriting is superb, and the team of Lennon and McCartney is truly on its game.

While they were writing and recording *Rubber Soul*, they had to have known that they were creating a masterpiece. All four Beatles have said in subsequent interviews that *Rubber Soul* was the first album on which they felt they took control in the studio. They were by now dab hands at the recording process, but they wanted a bigger say in how that music was recorded and mixed. The music comes pouring out of your headphones in ebullient, confident cascades of sound.

This is the last Beatles album on which Lennon appears to be the undisputed dominant force in the group. Always the unofficial leader of the band, his looming presence and force of personality can be felt even on those songs on which he is not the lead vocalist. Lyrically, *Rubber Soul* is Lennon's finest hour.

McCartney, on the other hand, seems to be catching up in terms of both producing radio-ready pop songs and molding his reputation as the greatest rock and roll bass player of all time. For the first time, we get to hear McCartney's bass driving the songs in a completely unconventional style of playing, and to reward his efforts, George Martin finally allows the bass track it's long overdue uptick in the mix.

Harrison turns in his two best songs to date, and shows that he doesn't have to resort to tepid rockabilly covers to claim a spot on an album. His chiming guitar is prominent throughout.

Starr has a lot more to do on *Rubber Soul* than he ever did before. Oddly syncopated beats and time signature changes abound on *Rubber Soul*, and Starr does what he does best: He augments the overall sound of the band, rather than overwhelm it with intrusive stick work.

"Drive My Car": Easily the tastiest chunk of rock and roll on *Rubber Soul*, "Drive My Car" seems almost out of place here. Sure, it leads off the album, but not once in the 13 songs that follow do the Beatles rock out like they do here. The insistent and obtrusive cowbell that clangs throughout the song and the hissy maracas are a tad distracting, but the guitar and bass playing the same hooky line chug this song along in urgent fashion. McCartney plays the piano figure that only appears during the chorus and the fade-out. The cowbell, piano and lead vocals appear all the way right in the stereo spectrum, as does the lead guitar solo. The line that ends each verse has Lennon doubled all the way to the left, another sign that George Martin was becoming invested in the notion of stereo mixes. During the second verse, McCartney's voice cracks badly on the word "time." Lennon's low harmony is guttural throughout, and at times it seems like he's having trouble keeping up with McCartney's lead vocal. At the 1:42 mark in the song, someone mumbles a word buried deep in the mix that is unintelligible. "Drive My Car" is one of the Beatles' most underrated soul-inflected songs.

"Norwegian Wood (This Bird Has Flown)": Much has been made of the fact that the Beatles incorporated a sitar into a pop song for the first time, but that is not really the primary triumph of this song. Perhaps no other song in rock and roll history captures a feel and nuance more succinctly and powerfully in 2:05 than "Norwegian Wood." Lennon's masterpiece is the best song on *Rubber Soul*, and remains a paragon of simplicity and craft. Lennon's acoustic guitar, wet with reverb, opens the song all the way over to the right, which is precisely where his world-weary lead vocal resides. Both have a distant, almost funereal sound, which gives the song the gravitas it demands. The simple bass, the sitar and, surprisingly, a second acoustic guitar appear on the left of the stereo spectrum. McCartney's harmony vocal lends an apt counterpart to Lennon's lead vocal, which is surprisingly low in the overall mix. In some ways, the sitar sounds cheesy and amateurish, but it does lend a certain individuality to the song. A muted floor bass drum accompanies the parts that Lennon and McCartney sing together. A tambourine makes its only appearance during the last verse. "Norwegian Wood" is one of the best songs the Beatles ever wrote and recorded. It's timeless and haunting, and stands as a telling document of where John Lennon's genius resided at the time.

"You Won't See Me": Unlike the rest of the songs on the album, "You Won't See Me" has a low-fi sound to it that makes it sound like it's coming out of a transistor radio. This belies the fact that "You Won't See Me" has the most inventive stereo mix on the entire album. First, you have McCartney's lead vocal panned all the way right, matched nicely with his own harmony vocal on the title line, which is then repeated by a backing trio of Lennon, Harrison *and* McCartney. The lead vocal puts the emphasis on the word "won't" while the backing vocals emphasize "see." The bridge has McCartney singing harmony with his lead vocal, while Lennon comes in with "knew I wouldn't..." in sort of an understated counterpoint. The "ooh la la las" dodge in and out of both channels, and someone (probably Lennon) singing that part sounds very hoarse during the last verse. The piano, guitar and bass are all panned way left; the instrumentation is spare, but the bass, while buried too deeply in the mix, is really unusual, and we can hear Starr doing triplets on his hi hat. Listen for sneaky hand claps on the outro only.

"Nowhere Man": No other original song recorded by the Beatles is as soaked in reverb as "Nowhere Man," at least on this version of the song. The effect is akin to a choir singing a capella in the narthex of a church. All the vocals are panned right, including Lennon's double-tracked lead vocal. The bass, drums, acoustic guitar and electric guitar are all the way to the left (just like the old days), although the acoustic moves slightly toward the center of the mix as the song progresses. The electric guitar solo happens just 47 seconds into the song, the earliest appearance of a guitar solo in any Beatles song. The solo is positioned all the way to the right in the stereo spectrum. McCartney, Harrison and Lennon are all singing the "la la la las," just mere minutes after we heard them singing "ooh la la las" in the previous song. Listen for the electric guitar on the left to appear only during the last two measures of each verse. McCartney shifts into a higher harmony on the last line of the song.

"Think for Yourself": Let's dispense with the housekeeping first: The word "rectify" just doesn't belong in a rock and roll song. Harrison's first cut on the album has a snaky beat not typical of most Harrison compositions. The electric piano and "fuzz" bass (really just a regular bass played through a blown amp) are all the way to the right, while the electric guitars and drums are all the way left. It was very unusual for instruments to be all over the map in the stereo picture during this era of the Beatles' career. Harrison's lead vocal is double-tracked (also very unusual) and it sounds like he has a bit of a head cold. Lennon and McCartney's harmony leaks into both channels, and lends a bluesy flavor to the last line.

"The Word": "The Word" is one of the happiest sounding Beatles songs ever, and also one of the simplest. Over an arrangement of piano, guitar, bass and drums, Lennon, McCartney and Harrison exercise their vocal chops and extol the virtues of love, which turns out to be "the word." The piano, guitar and one harmony vocal are all the way left, while the other two vocals and the bass are panned to the right. And do check out the bass; although it's once again buried too deeply in the mix, it propels this song along with purpose and exigency. The appearance of a second electric guitar occurs only during the verses. The maracas are played throughout the song. During the final chorus, McCartney adds a scintillating high harmony that lifts the song to new heights. Check out the spastic organ at the end of the song.

"Michelle": "Michelle" is a marvel of economy, both in its playing and singing. Two acoustic guitars play identical figures during the intro (and double each other every other time that figure appears in the song), but the second guitar does not appear during the verses. McCartney's lead vocal is all the way right, and the wordless syllables sung by Lennon and Harrison are mixed way over to the left. The bass appears under the backing vocals on the left, while the low-key drums are under McCartney's vocal on the right. Both electric guitar solos are remarkable for their restraint and mellow tones. It's only during the outro that one can hear the second acoustic guitar play a quick upstroke on the corresponding chord. Check it out at 2:29.

"What Goes On": A low-budget "Act Naturally," "What Goes On" finds Starr mining his Buck Owens jones for a discordant (and poorly played) pseudo-country song. It has all the requisite ingredients—love lost, lying, infidelity, plus the wounded crooning of its slightly out-of-tune singer—but it's all been done before. And way better than this. Lennon and Harrison man the electric guitars, with Lennon's sounding very out of tune. For some reason, the electric guitars are mixed way too high and overwhelm the rest of the instrumentation. Besides, they're clunky, ham-handed and not played very well. Even Harrison's Carl Perkins–inflected solo sounds pallid and uninteresting. Starr's vocal is all the way to the left. Lennon and McCartney add wordless backing vocals on the right side. Drums and bass are all the way left, and the guitars all the way right. After the second "tell me why," you can hear Starr repeat the line very quietly. The song speeds up slightly during the last chorus, and if you listen very closely, you can hear Starr repeat the final phrase twice before the song ends.

"Girl": This is a very interesting song, not only because of its intricate structure and mature lyrics, but also because of its time changes and seductive guitar parts. Lennon's vocal is double-tracked all the way right in the mix, while his capoed acoustic guitar appears all the way left, along with the bass and drums. The "ah, girl..." hook doesn't sound like it was followed by a sigh, which is what conventional wisdom holds. A sigh is an exhalation, and this is most definitely an inhalation. They were doing a lot of inhaling in this period. Harrison and McCartney singing the naughty "tit tit tit tit" backing to the bridge is clever, but I would have preferred to suss it out on my own, rather than have the boys clue me in. A second acoustic guitar appears during the last verse, and a third plays a wild accompaniment on the waltzy measures before the outro. Lennon's first mention of the word "dead" appears in this song. "Girl" is a tremendous song and one of the most underrated compositions in the Beatles catalog.

"I'm Looking Through You": A strange tune and one that sounds like no other song the Beatles recorded. It's driven totally by an acoustic guitar—played by McCartney—so high in the mix that it dominates even the bass, drums, electric guitar and the pointless organ they showed Starr how to play on this session. The drums and guitar are all the way left, and McCartney's double-tracked vocal is all the way right. There is also this weird frenetic tapping sound underlying the whole thing, as if someone is slapping an empty cardboard box. McCartney belts out some bluesy lines on the fade-out.

"In My Life": As if "Norwegian Wood" and "Girl" weren't enough, Lennon turns in this lovely reminiscence of his life thus far, complete with baroque musical undertones and a frantic piano solo (played by George Martin) that sounds like it was forcibly wedged into the limited measures the song's instrumental break allowed for. Lennon's double-tracked lead vocal, ably augmented by McCartney and Harrison's harmony vocals, are shoved over all the way right, while the electric guitars, bass and drums reside on the left in the mix. Very Starr-like playing, with the trap on his snare drum off. Lennon's falsetto on the final "In my life," adds the right dose of drama. In another band's hands, "In My Life" could have been a really maudlin song, but the confluence of the Beatles' good taste and beautiful harmonies turn it into a celebration. Second use of the word "dead."

"Wait": One of the few times in their early- to mid-period that the Beatles dusted off a song meant for a previous album, "Wait" was recorded during the *Help!* sessions. They added it to *Rubber Soul* at the last minute. It's a subtly complex song. Lennon and McCartney's vocals are all the way to the right, where they have to contend with a tambourine and maracas that vie for the spotlight. Also, an electric guitar appears on the right. The other electric guitar is mixed left with the bass and drums. Both Lennon and McCartney's vocals are double-tracked. If you listen very closely to "Wait," it does sound like it fits better on *Help!* than *Rubber Soul*.

"If I Needed Someone": This is Harrison's second contribution to *Rubber Soul*, and a far superior one than the first. The ringing electric guitars and close harmonies cast a rosy glow over what is really a thinly veiled song about infidelity. Harrison's lead vocal is double tracked and wet with reverb, two recording tricks he most decidedly did not favor. Again, voices to the right and instruments to the left. The only exception to this is during the instrumental break, when a third electric guitar echoes the riff and wanders slightly into right channel territory. Lennon and McCartney's harmony vocals almost completely overwhelm Harrison's lead vocal. Listen for a tambourine to sneak into the mix on the right during the outro.

"Run for Your Life": Why they chose to close *Rubber Soul* with a song that seems to be about domestic violence is puzzling. Lennon gets in his last recitation of the word "dead," at least on this album. All the instruments are positioned all the way left. Five seconds into the song, you can hear whoever is working the board at the session literally pot up the right channel to open the track for the vocalist. It's fascinating to hear this, and right on cue, here comes Lennon's menacing lead vocal. An odd thing about the backing vocals: All three of them are singing backing vocals, but McCartney's and Harrison's are mixed right, while Lennon's is mixed left. Both the guitar solo and the pseudo-slide guitar are on the right side of the mix. During the fade-out the first electric guitar starts making forays onto the right side of the stereo picture.

Revolver

RELEASED AUGUST 5, 1966

"We would go through the complete range of EQ on a disc, and if that wasn't enough, we'd put it through another range of EQ again, multiplied, and we'd get the most weird sound, which the Beatles like and which obviously worked."

—*George Martin*[12]

"I felt we were progressing in leaps and bounds, musically. It was getting to be really exciting in the studio. We did it all in there: rehearsing, recording and finishing songs. We never hired a rehearsal room to run down the songs, because a lot of them weren't finished."

—*Ringo Starr*[13]

"I'd bring Paul's bass forward in the mix to give it more presence, because having been involved in mastering records, I was used to hearing American singles with a higher level of bass on them. I used a loudspeaker on "Paperback Writer"—I thought if a loudspeaker can push bass out, then it can pull the bass in."

—*Geoff Emerick*[14]

Revolver captures the Beatles at their very best and by almost any measure is their finest album. It's on this album that the Beatles once and for all took over in the studio, urging George Martin to find exotic and experimental sounds that hadn't been widely employed on any rock and roll album to date.

The album was released just weeks before the last live concert they played, ending a whirlwind four-year schedule of breakneck travel, with all its attendant complications. Henceforth, the Beatles could take their time in the recording studio, harnessing their creative energy and synthesizing it into even more interesting songs.

Revolver was an important stepping stone into this new era of creativity sans touring. Beatlemania wasn't exactly dead, but legions of faithful fans would eventually wonder what they were up to and whether they were still a viable band in the rock firmament. *Revolver* was a tempting harbinger of what was yet to come.

To give proper context to the maturity and complexity of *Revolver* as a work of rock and roll significance, one only has to consider what the pop charts looked liked during the week it was released. Two of the top ten hits during that week were novelty songs so lightweight that you could almost see them float away forever ("Winchester Cathedral" by the New Vaudeville Band, and "Lady Godiva" by Peter and Gordon, who had previously recorded a Lennon-McCartney reject, "World Without Love"), and two other songs were recorded by artists that your parents probably favored ("Born Free" by Roger Williams, and "That's Life" by Frank Sinatra).

Chockfull of crunchy electric guitars, oddly syncopated beats, generous helpings of horns and strings, backwards guitar and random tape loops, *Revolver* also contained some of their most tuneful songs and easily their most skillfully played music. The band was in full flower and in complete communion with each other. This is the Beatles album you would play to a person who had never heard their music. It emphasizes their best qualities (rich melodies, exquisite harmonies, tasty guitar work and some of their best lyrics), while eschewing some of their lesser tendencies (the occasional mawkish deep album track and an idle amble down music hall lane).

Ten months later, the Beatles would release *Sgt. Pepper's Lonely Hearts Club Band* to great critical acclaim, but *Revolver* is a better album overall. *Sgt. Pepper* was really a vehicle for Paul McCartney to express his varied musical tastes in the guise of a band setting. On some tracks on *Sgt. Pepper*, George Harrison doesn't even appear and John Lennon is relegated to shaking a tambourine. Conversely, *Revolver* finds a shared division of musical craft and sensibility between McCartney and Lennon, with a huge assist from Harrison. Moreover, the presence of all four Beatles can either be heard or intuited on every song on *Revolver*.

More than this, the songs are just better on *Revolver*. From chamber music to psychedelia, from a Stax-inflected rave-up to a fond nod to the Beach Boys, it's all here. This is really the only Beatles album that doesn't contain at least one average song. All 14 songs on *Revolver* are studies in extremely tasteful song craft and innovative musicianship.

Never again would the band be so totally in synch with each other; each of their subsequent albums were significant musical achievements in their own right, but none would capture the pure and unassailable magic of *Revolver*.

This is the last album on which John Lennon plays the dominant role in the group. He's the lead singer (and songwriter) on five tracks here, and his guitar playing is as good as it's ever been (and ever would be). Four of his five tracks feature loud, acid-tinged electric guitars. This is also one of the only Beatles albums on which Lennon's vocals are not subjected to heavy reverb and tinctures of echo.

McCartney was the chief songwriter on six of the songs, and the lead singer on five of those. He seems to have developed a predilection for a melding of chamber music with pop balladry, and he uses that formula to great effect on two tracks on *Revolver*. His bass playing is typically inventive, and his clear tenor sounds as good here as it ever has.

Harrison had his busiest album to date: He contributed three songs to *Revolver*, and for the first and only time, a Harrison-penned tune was the opening track on a Beatles album. He also contributed some of his finest guitar playing with the Beatles.

Ringo Starr gets his obligatory novelty song to sing, but this one is among his best. His more significant contribution to *Revolver* is a heavy drum sound that ably complements the tremendous songs his three bandmates brought to the studio.

"Taxman": This savory chunk of English rock and roll has a pretty straightforward mix. After a few seconds of coughing and counting, the song blasts out of the headphones with a stridency that is undeniable. Harrison's electric guitar, the bass and drums are all the way left, while the lead and backing vocals are centered. Oddly, the backing vocals are moved right for the third verse only, after which they are centered again. The right channel features a cowbell and McCartney's searing electric guitar solo, played on his Epiphone Casino. A tambourine is evident starting with the second verse. On the last verse, McCartney doubles Harrison's guitar riff until the solo returns during the song's fade-out. It seems likely that George Martin cut and pasted McCartney's first solo onto the fade-out, as the two are indistinguishable, and would have been difficult for even the most skilled guitarist to duplicate note for note.

"Eleanor Rigby": An epic accomplishment of simplicity and melancholy, interwoven with two string quartets recorded twice over, "Eleanor Rigby" sounded like nothing else on the airwaves at the time. On this mix, the strings are all the way left (although they occasionally veer toward the center later in the song), with McCartney's lead vocal—regrettably—pushed all the way to the right. (This mixing flaw would be rectified on the *Yellow Submarine* soundtrack album two years later).

72

The first word of the song can be heard in the middle of the mix, but is quickly corrected for the rest of the song (an engineer probably forgot to turn off the ADT). The backing vocals are all the way left (all accounts of this song's recording credit Lennon and Harrison with the backing vocals, but if they did sing on this song, it's not very evident; future mixes of "Eleanor Rigby" would put this question to the test once again). McCartney alone sings the backing vocals on the last chorus. His lead vocal is centered on the choruses and doubled.

"I'm Only Sleeping": Lennon's somnambulant tendencies crop up again here. (He mentions sleep in "A Hard Day's Night" and would build an entire song around that theme on the *White Album*.) Lennon's lead vocal appears on both channels, with drums, bass and acoustic guitar on the left. The bass plays a simple figure solo that introduces the bridges, and that is centered. The bass is pretty much buried during the rest of the song. The backing vocals appear between the center and right in the stereo picture. A loud backwards electric guitar is the main feature of the instrumental break, and appears again during the song's coda. Listen for McCartney's yawn at 2:00.

"Love You To": Harrison's first full-on Indian music effort is among his best. His voice sounds clear and the melody is interesting. A tamboura and sitars, plus various Indian percussion instruments, flood both channels with a wall of Eastern instrumentation. A muted electric guitar can be heard occasionally in the middle of the mix. Harrison's lead vocal is doubled and can be heard on the left and right. A harmony vocal, sung by Harrison, can be heard in the center of the mix at the end of every verse.

"Here, There and Everywhere": A beautiful melody (and sentiment) built around an ascending chord sequence that veers in and out of three different keys. McCartney's doubled lead vocal can be heard on both channels and is treated to a bit of an acceleration using varispeed. The wordless backing vocals, sung by Lennon and Harrison, give the melody an understated drama. An electric guitar playing the staccato chords is all the way right, where you can also find a very hushed drum part. A second doubled electric guitar playing a countermelody can be heard left and right during the two bridges. McCartney's voice cracks at 1:34. Listen for finger snaps to begin at 1:55 (but the third one is inexplicably missing).

"Yellow Submarine": This nautically based romp has a plethora of sea sounds, background merry-making and a few measures of a brass band, all centered in the mix. The drums, acoustic guitar, bass and maracas are all the way left, while Starr's lead vocal and the very enthusiastic backing vocals are on the right. The backing vocals also move to the left during the last chorus only. Listen for Lennon and McCartney to voice the seaman's instructions during the instrumental break, and then Lennon—in his very best British Royal Navy voice—echoing Starr's lines during the final verse.

"She Said She Said": A cachophony of loud, crunchy electric guitars—all the way to the right in the mix—introduces this song that was purportedly written about an acid trip Lennon took in Los Angeles. Tricky time signatures give this song an oddly syncopated tug-and-pull. The bass and drums are all the way left, with Starr making good use of his crash symbols in spots. The lead and backing vocals are centered and all sung by Lennon. The one exception is during the fade-out, when Harrison echoes Lennon's lines. It has been written that McCartney did not appear on this track, and that seems likely, as the bass used here is not the Rickenbacker he was playing during this time period, and lacks the sort of melodicism that was his hallmark during this period. It's clear also that McCartney doesn't sing on this track. If this is indeed true, it's one of the only songs in the entire catalogue that doesn't include McCartney.

"Good Day Sunshine": While not the best song on the album, "Good Day Sunshine" is certainly one of the most interesting to listen to on headphones. There are two separate drum parts, and two separate piano parts, one each on the left and right. The piano on the left is played by McCartney, while the piano on the right—including the saloon-style solo—is played by George Martin. Starr's main drum part is on the left, while his cymbal crashes appear on the right, starting seven seconds into the song. The lead and backing vocals appear centered, except during the fade-out, when they move from right to left and then back again. The handclaps only appear during the final verse. Listen for Lennon to murmur a one-syllable word at 1:25 deep in the mix, after which McCartney seems to be trying to stifle a chuckle.

"And Your Bird Can Sing": This song includes one of the most complicated guitar lines to ever grace a Beatles tune. It's doubled by two guitarists (probably Harrison and McCartney) and moves the song along in a propulsive manner. The lead and backing vocals can be heard on both channels, while a rhythm guitar and drums can be heard on the left. The drums can also be heard on the right, along with a tambourine. The bass is centered, and handclaps dodge in and out of the mix. This is a tremendous song and wholly representative of the Beatles overall sound at the time.

"For No One": Easily the saddest Beatles song ever, "For No One" expresses feelings of lost love and missed chances that most everyone has experienced at some time in their lives. Set to a stark accompaniment dominated by a clavichord played by McCartney, it's haunting and lovely at the same time. The bass and a tambourine can be heard on the left, where the beautiful French horn solo also appears, first during the instrumental break, and then again under McCartney's vocal on the last verse. Muted drums can be heard on the right channel, with McCartney's lead vocal right smack dab in the middle.

"Dr. Robert": Very similar to "And Your Bird Can Sing" and "She Said She Said" in tone and feel, "Dr. Robert" includes some interesting time signature changes that disrupt the flow of the song. One electric guitar, drums and maracas are centered, while Lennon's double-tracked lead vocal can be heard on both channels. McCartney sings a very effective harmony vocal that also appears in both channels. Two additional electric guitars are on the left and right, with an organ all the way right during the bridges. Listen for the speeded up outro that actually has a cold ending before it completely fades out.

"I Want to Tell You": Harrison's third and final song on the album has an interesting, old school mix. Most of the instruments are on the left, and most of the vocals are on the right. Electric guitar, drums, piano and maracas appear on the left, along with some (but not all) of the backing vocals. On the right, one can hear the bass, the doubled lead vocal and still more backing vocals. Handclaps appear throughout the song. Harrison's lead vocal gets moved to the center on the last verse only. The electric guitar also moves slightly toward the center as the song progresses. This song includes a complex vocal mélange on the fade-out, a technique they also used on "She Said She Said" and "Good Day Sunshine."

"Got to Get You Into My Life": One of the few Beatles songs to feature horns played in a style much closer to soul music than classical,

"Got to Get You Into My Life" is an energetic rocker that doesn't rely on electric guitars for its drive. The horns are the only instruments found on the right channel, while the drums and bass are on the left. Listen closely and you will also hear an electric guitar on the left, potted down so low in the mix as to be almost inaudible. At 1:44, one full note of an electric guitar sneaks into the center of the mix, before two very loud electric guitars come in full bore at 1:48. An organ can also be heard, but only during the fade-out. McCartney's lead vocal is doubled only on the title phrase.

"Tomorrow Never Knows": The closing track on *Revolver* is awash with weird sounds, random tape loops, backwards guitar and manipulated vocals. The bass, drums and haunting lead vocal by Lennon appear in the center of the mix. Tape loops are all the way left, while the right channel is overloaded with cymbals, organ, backwards electric guitar and a tambourine that doesn't make its first appearance until the 1:49 mark. A doubled lead vocal can also be heard on the right. A piano comes in at 2:43 and plays through the face-out. Lennon's vocal on the last verse is run through an amp speaker to give it a distant, tinny quality. It's a sure bet the Beatles purposely made "Tomorrow Never Knows" the last cut on *Revolver* to foreshadow what was to come. Finally, off the road and in the studio for keeps, they soon would have more musical surprises to spring on the world.

Sgt. Pepper's Lonely Hearts Club Band
RELEASED JUNE 2, 1967

"Looking back on Pepper, you can see it was quite an icon. It was the record of that time, and it probably did change the face of recording; but we didn't do it consciously. I think there was a gradual development by the boys, as they tried to make life a bit more interesting on record.... It became a different kind of art form—like making a film rather than a live performance."

—*George Martin*[15]

"At that stage, we had just discovered stereo, so we panned everything everywhere. I remember we asked why there were always little breaks between songs on a record. The engineers told us they were traditionally three seconds long, and they were there so the DJs could get their records lined up. We thought, 'You could put something in there, little funny sounds.' And then we heard the engineers talking about frequencies, and we asked about them. They said, 'Well, you've got low and high frequencies. Only your dog can hear the highest ones.' We said, 'You're kidding.' Then they told us that people had experimented with low frequencies as weapons—you can blow a city away if the frequency is strong enough. So we thought, 'Well, we've got to have a bit that only dogs can hear. Why make records for humans?'"

—*Paul McCartney*[16]

Much has been written about *Sgt. Pepper's Lonely Hearts Club Band*. No rock and roll album has ever been dissected more assiduously. The prevailing consensus among rock historians is that it is a work of epic span and gravity, and that it completely changed rock and roll forever.

I regard it in a less reverent light. While certainly innovative and ahead of its time, it hasn't aged very well. It's chockfull of tape manipulation and other studio chicanery. Listening to McCartney's voice on "When I'm Sixty-Four" and "Lovely Rita" gives the impression that the singer is a 16-year-old with a lovely Irish tenor in development. Lennon's voice on "Lucy in the Sky with Diamonds" is so speeded up that he sounds downright pre-pubescent. No doubt part of their fondness for tape speed variances was rooted in their experimentation with mind-altering substances, but one wonders what those songs would have sounded like in their original, real-time form.

Still, this is a quibble. The songs—for the most part—are inventive and interesting to listen to on headphones. In fact, *Sgt. Pepper* is one of the most interesting Beatles albums to listen to with the cans strapped on.

It's by far their most "British" album. Their accents seem more pronounced and the lyrics are filled with references to English locales: Blackburn, Lancashire, Bishopsgate, the Isle of Wight, Albert Hall … it's a veritable tour of the British Isles. Even British idioms ("dear" as a synonym for "expensive") make the scene.

This is Paul McCartney's shining moment as a Beatle. His songwriting craft dominates this album and his inventive bass playing adds a remarkable low end to the songs that cannot be underestimated, and that was subsequently excessively cribbed by bass players in other high-profile rock bands. Henceforward, McCartney dominated the remaining Beatles albums.

John Lennon, on the other hand, seems almost a bemused passenger on the *Sgt. Pepper* bus. He is the chief author of the best song on the album—"A Day in the Life"—but the other songs he offered up seem lazy and disingenuous (with the exception of "Lucy in the Sky with Diamonds"). At the time of the album's recording, he was living a banal existence as a young millionaire husband and father. His creative juices dulled by the ennui of suburban domestic life, he only grudgingly accepted the prospect of his participation in this project. In fact, his appearances as a guitar player on this album are extremely limited.

George Harrison is almost completely absent from the proceedings. Other than the two "Sgt. Pepper's," his own contribution to the album and "A Day in the Life," Harrison's presence cannot be heard nor even intuited. On a couple of the songs, McCartney plays the guitar solos, a role Harrison usually filled.

This is Ringo Starr's best album as the Beatles' drummer. Inventive fills, increased use of his floor bass, and less reliance on his ride cymbals give the album the necessary percussive element it cries for.

The instrumentation on the album is typically inventive. No studio prop was neglected in the making of the album. What is especially interesting is the almost total lack of acoustic guitars, just two albums removed from their most acoustic-heavy album, *Rubber Soul*. Acoustic guitars appear on just three songs in the whole set, and only on the album's closer does an acoustic play a prominent role.

"Sgt. Pepper's Lonely Hearts Club Band": George Martin goes over the top in his desire to make this a stereo-heavy LP. McCartney's lead vocals can barely be heard; they're mixed so far to the right as to be almost off the scale of the stereo picture. The fake crowd noises, the horns and the backing vocals are panned all the way to the left. The lead guitar appears in the center of the stereo spectrum, but fades away almost completely during the last verse. The lead guitar is on the right, and the bass and booming drums are centered.

"With a Little Help from My Friends": Great vocal by Starr, maybe his best. The first time Lennon and McCartney come in is the only time, other than on "Carry That Weight" on *Abbey Road*, that they both sing the same part as a backing vocal. Listen for the added double-tracked lead vocal as Starr attempts to finish the song with a flourish. The piano, electric guitar and drums are centered, while the bass, tambourine and lead guitar are pushed right. Listen for Starr to lightly ride his cymbals on the last verse only.

"Lucy in the Sky with Diamonds": It's slightly distracting that Lennon's vocals (although not McCartney's harmony) are speeded up. Lennon's vocal is double-tracked only on the last lines of the three verses. Listen closely right after the word "high." Lennon sings "high" again, as if to make the point even more obvious. A harpsichord-sounding keyboard—actually a Mellotron—and the drums are all the way left, while the bass and an electric guitar with a wobbly effect are on the right. Listen for a guttural "oh" at 3:23 during the fade-out.

"Getting Better": A mind-blowing song, in terms of its meter changes and its harmonies. The congas are on the right, along with an electric guitar and intermittent handclaps. A piano also appears on the right, but only during the second verse. A second guitar is all the way right, along with an electric piano and drums. This song includes some of the Beatles' best harmonies.

"Fixing a Hole": Conventional wisdom has it that Harrison played the guitar solo (he doesn't; it's McCartney playing almost the same solo he played on "Taxman," and, by the way, using the same guitar, his Epiphone Casino) and that Harrison and Lennon sang the background vocals. Harrison's voice does not appear on this track; it's all Lennon and McCartney. McCartney's heavily reverbed double-tracked vocal cracks noticeably at the end of the "go." Backing vocals and an electric guitar are all the way right, while the harpsichord, bass and drums are all the way left. Listen for the bass flub at 2:15. When we deconstruct the mono albums, you'll note that the backing vocals on this track are almost completely absent.

"She's Leaving Home": Something happens in this song that almost never occurs in other Beatles songs written by McCartney: His voice is double-tracked during the chorus. And it's not the fake double-tracking that they so often employed; he's singing twice. So is Lennon, but that was routine at this point. Lennon's second vocal decays sooner than the first, and McCartney uncharacteristically falls off key on "our baby's gone." During the choruses one voice each from Lennon and McCartney can be heard on both channels. The harp is all the way right, while strings can be heard on both sides of the stereo spectrum.

"Being for the Benefit of Mr. Kite": Lennon's vocal is mixed so far to the right as to be almost indistinguishable. His vocal is triple-tracked, something they never did before. Martin has gated the reverb so there is no lingering effect. It's an interesting choice, but overused in this case. It's only at the end of the line that immediately precedes the wild instrumental break that Lennon's vocal is quickly panned to the center of the mix. Lead and backing vocals are all the way right, as are the Mellotron, several different organs and an electric guitar. On the left you hear the bass, another organ and the cascading carousel-like sounds during the outro.

"Within You Without You": Unsurprisingly, this is the song that seems most out of place on this album. Harrison's vocal is strong and assured, and the melody isn't bad at all. George Martin couldn't resist added some Western strings to the Eastern instrumentation. In the middle of the song, there is a frenetic and long instrumental break; just before Harrison begins to sing again you can hear someone say "dah, dah, dah, one two," as if to count him back in. Strangely, it sounds like McCartney. Of course, the bizarre few seconds of laughter after the song ends adds some much-needed comic relief before the next song begins in less than one full second.

"When I'm 64": It's so obvious that this was recorded prior to the official *Sgt. Pepper* sessions, because it's the cleanest song on the LP. There are no broken chords, strained vocals or slight meter mishaps. It's almost too clean. The backing vocals are Lennon and Harrison and can be heard all the way right, where the oboes and clarinet also reside in the mix. Check out the understated electric guitar that doesn't make its appearance till the end of the last verse, at 2:10. McCartney's speeded up lead vocal and some chimes are all the way left, while the bulk of the instruments (drums, bass and piano) are centered.

"Lovely Rita": This is the best "stereo" song on the LP. This one also points out the limitations of recording on four-track; it's too separated. Again, absolutely no sign of Harrison and other than the backing track, Lennon isn't playing, either. The backing vocals are soaked with reverb. It's George Martin playing the brief piano solo, under which you can also here a faint organ that only appears in the mix during the piano solo. On the phrase "over dinner" you can hear someone make a loud popping sound with his mouth. Someone can be heard blowing bubbles in a container of water at :32. The "chick-a, chick-a, chick-a" sound heard two lines into each verse is McCartney vocalizing what sounds a bit like a percussive instrument. Acoustic guitar, drums and piano are all the way left, while a separate piano playing the solo can be heard, along with the bass guitar, on the right channel. The backing vocals move all over the stereo picture during the outro.

"Good Morning, Good Morning": Again, it's McCartney playing the guitar solo. It's too "Taxman"-like not to be McCartney, and besides, in the backing tracks, you can't hear Harrison at all. Unlike other vocals sung by Lennon on this album, here his vocal is completely dry, unfettered by the reverb and echo he favored. He's triple-tracked only on the last verse. Listen for Starr playing sneaky triplets on the fadeout. An electric guitar, drums and bass are all the way left, while the horns, backing vocals and handclaps are all the way right. Lennon's lead vocal is centered, and he occasionally harmonizes with himself. The electric guitar solo is also centered. When listening to the animal sounds during the fade-out, you can hear the sound of horses trotting moving from right to left.

"Sgt. Pepper's Lonely Hearts Club Band (Reprise)": Much better mix than the opening song, with the vocals being more centered. The very first electric guitar note is on the left, but quickly centered. During the count in, you can hear someone who sounds like Harrison say "bye-ee." This time the vocals are in unison and centered in the mix; the fake crowd noises are almost non-existent. After the last "Hearts … Club … Band," you can hear deep in the mix on the left McCartney saying very quickly "thank you very much everybody." I'd like to know why they buried Paul. The vocals are on the left, and the drums on the right, with all the other instruments (two electric guitars, bass and the very occasional crowd noises) being centered.

"A Day in the Life": This is by far the best song on the album. It's McCartney on bass and piano, Lennon on piano, Harrison on acoustic and Starr on drums. The reverb on Lennon's voice is over the top. Even though this is principally Lennon's song, McCartney's middle eight is among the most interesting parts of this song, especially since his vocal is delivered completely dry, in stark contrast to Lennon's vocal. You can hear McCartney say "one" just before he starts singing. Lennon's vocal starts all the way to the right and slowly pans center and then left as the song progresses. The piano and acoustic guitar are panned all the way left to begin the song, and make their way to the far right before the song ends, passing Lennon's vocal on their trek across the stereo spectrum. This is the second album in a row on which the closing song does not contain the title in the lyrics.

Magical Mystery Tour

RELEASED ON NOVEMBER 27, 1967

> "Working with them as a training engineer was incredible because you couldn't really do too much wrong with The Beatles. You had the perfect set up for experimenting to find mics you liked. It wasn't a typical three-hour session where you had an orchestra and you had to do two songs in a three-hour session—where you had the pressure, so you had to get it right from the get-go. With The Beatles, they were spending ages. They loved experimentation, so that gave you the freedom to try things."
>
> —Ken Scott[17]

Magical Mystery Tour is one of the oddest albums in the entire Beatles catalogue. Ostensibly, it was meant to be a six-song EP of the songs that appeared in the film of the same name, and it was released in that format in England and other European countries. For American audiences, of course, EPs were not a viable format option, so Capitol padded the original film song track with five songs that had been previously released as singles earlier in 1967.

While the Magical Mystery Tour film was excoriated by critics (marking the first time any Beatles product had been roundly criticized), the album received the usual plaudits and was nominated for a Grammy award. It was a clear message that the Beatles should stick with what they do best: making ground-breaking music of epic innovation and style. It was a message they would fail to heed on at least two other occasions during their career.

The album is oddly bifurcated: The six songs that appeared in the film—with two notable exceptions—are average compositions that one wouldn't play as a way of introduction to someone who had never heard the Beatles' music. The mixes are for the most part interesting, and the Beatles once again explored the use of non-traditional rock and roll instruments to give the songs color, but the songs themselves just aren't very good. In addition, the album contains an inordinate complement of horns and, to a slightly lesser degree, strings. Alternative keyboard instruments—Mellotrons and a clavioline (a sort of prototype synthesizer)—abound.

Conversely, the five songs that were previously released as singles shine with a pristine complexity and a singular elegance. This album was released almost exactly six months after their opus, *Sgt. Pepper's Lonely Hearts Club Band,* and in fact contained two songs that were the first songs the band recorded during the *Sgt. Pepper* sessions. The difference in quality between the soundtrack songs and the previous singles is undeniably obvious.

In some ways, *Magical Mystery Tour* is the son of *Sgt. Pepper.* Both were based on grandiose ideas in which the Beatles would shed their identities and bury them in a pretense: a faux band for *Sgt. Pepper* and, in the case of *Magical Mystery Tour,* a capricious fantasy (a bus tour with an odd assortment of colorful common folk—none of whom the Beatles would be likely to hobnob with in their real lives).

Both albums were primarily Paul McCartney's brainchildren. *Magical Mystery Tour* is the first album the Beatles made after the August 1967 death of their manager, Brian Epstein, and the first subtle hints of dissension within the band began to foment during the making of the album and the film.

McCartney, for his part, produced two excellent songs ("The Fool on the Hill" and "Penny Lane") for this set, and his bass playing is even more inventive than ever. This is the third album in a row in which McCartney's songs were primarily piano-based; he seems to have forsaken the guitar for a short time during their middle period. From here on out, McCartney would dominate the Beatles remaining albums musically (much to the eventual chagrin of his bandmates).

John Lennon turns in just one song for the soundtrack, but it's the best song of the six they recorded for the film. He dominates the singles on the album, with three of the five being among the entire album's most interesting tunes. That the same album contains "I Am the Walrus," "Strawberry Fields Forever," and "All You Need Is Love"—three songs that perfectly define Lennon's incalculable contributions to the Beatles catalogue—makes *Magical Mystery Tour* (however flawed) a landmark musical achievement for the group and for Lennon. Still in all, on the five soundtrack songs that he didn't write, he sounds a bit like a semi-interested bystander.

George Harrison's sole contribution is maudlin, tepid and a little creepy sounding. Moreover, this album features just one Harrison guitar solo, and that one falls apart badly halfway through. Clearly, Harrison's role in the band was changing.

Ringo Starr's drumming throughout is big and brash, but he does not sing on any of the songs, except for the instrumental "Flying," on which all four Beatles sing. The band's democratic ethos of providing Starr with one song per album was bypassed on this album, chiefly because that ideal didn't quite fit within the constraints of recording a soundtrack for the film.

"Magical Mystery Tour": The title track crashes in with a cascade of drums, bass, piano and horns. The bass starts on the right channel but veers toward the center as the song progresses. Maracas, drums, electric guitar and piano stay on the left the entire song, until the fade-out, when you can faintly hear the tinkling of a second piano on the right channel. The horns are all the way right, where the lead vocal also resides (except for the introduction, when McCartney uses a carnival barker voice to announce the tour; that vocal is centered). The backing vocals are also centered. The occasional sounds of a bus roaring by move from right to left in the mix. Interestingly, McCartney sings the first two choruses, but Lennon is the lead singer on the third and final one. Listen for someone to murmur the word "yes" at 2:25.

"The Fool On the Hill": McCartney's best song on the album is dominated by three harmonicas, two flutes and a recorder, all heard on the right channel, except for the instrumental break, during which the flutes leech into the center of the mix. McCartney's superlative lead vocal is doubled on the chorus only and centered in the mix. A piano, acoustic guitar, tambourine and several other light percussive parts are all the way left. There is no bass guitar on this track, an unusual occurrence on a Beatles song that gets the full band treatment. A trio of bass harmonicas provides the lower end to the song. Listen for what sounds like yet another bus roll from left to right for two seconds at 2:40.

"Flying": What a weird song this is. There are no lyrics, just vocalized syllables sung lustily by all four band members, centered in the mix. The left is dominated by an electric guitar, bass, drums and organ, and the right channel has a very complicated acoustic guitar figure, accompanied by light tapping on the guitar that it's played on. Maracas also show up on the right. A Mellotron—an instrument they were extremely fond of during this period—is centered in the mix, and slides to the left during the long fade-out that also includes snippets of a backwards guitar.

To quote "Penny Lane": Very strange.

"Blue Jay Way": Harrison's sole contribution to the proceedings oozes with bathos and subterranean mysticism. From the opening strains of a dirge-like organ, the song grows to a crescendo of overly phased drums and vocals, with eerie backwards backing vocals. Listen for a light tapping on the left channel at the very start of the song. The organ, drums and bass are all the way left, while the strings, a heavily phased lead vocal and a tambourine are on the right. The backwards backing vocals (and a normal backing vocal on the chorus only) are accompanied in the center of the mix by a menacing sounding cello. Listen for a brief organ swell in the center at 3:34.

"Your Mother Should Know": This simple-sounding song features a very complex mix. The wordless vocals during the introduction are all over the mix (both left and right), while the piano and the bass are centered (although the bass occasionally veers to the right). Drums and organ are on the right, as are a quick couple of cymbal hits 20 seconds into the song. McCartney's lead vocal, and Lennon and Harrison's backing vocals are on the left during the first two verses, and you can hear all the instruments and voices come to the left at 1:43. Then, the vocals move all the way right for the third and final verse. The drums also appear on the right and center. McCartney sings the "dada dada" syllables near the end of the song as a sneaky counterpoint to a song that has "mother" in the title. The last word he sings is "know," after which Lennon and Harrison sing "yeah."

The wordless last verse has McCartney's vocals left and center, and the backing vocals in the center and left as well.

"I Am the Walrus": A Lennon tour de force of operatic proportions. The 2009 remastered release of *Magical Mystery Tour* includes two extra bars of the introduction, before the whole thing melds into a cacophony of apocalyptic sound. You can hear the right track opened at :03, followed immediately by the swell of noise provided by strings and horns. Starr's domineering drums come bashing in on the left, along with an electric guitar, bass and piano. Lennon's double-tracked lead vocal is centered, and over-modulates on the words "a row" at 1:09. The lead vocal leaks into the right channel, along with the backing vocals and the random snippets from a trip across the radio dial. And then, the revelation: At 2:11, the track goes from fake stereo to mono, suddenly and without warning. The long fade-out is panned from right to left, ever so slowly. This is easily the scariest Beatles song, rife with ominous sounding minor chords and nonsensical but somehow foreboding lyrics.

"Hello Goodbye": Back when record albums had "sides," one could easily hear the shift from soundtrack songs to previously recorded singles that split *Magical Mystery Tour* right down the middle. The songs on the "second side" sound more polished, a little less dark and certainly more radio-friendly. "Hello Goodbye" is a prime example of this. Emboldened by a strong McCartney lead vocal, and very supportive backing vocals by Lennon and Harrison, the song pours out of your headphones with a resonant optimism. The piano, drums, maracas and tambourine are all the way left, where an organ can also be heard on the last chorus only. The lead vocal and the bass are centered, while an electric guitar, strings, backing vocals and four handclaps (at 1:14) can be heard all the way right. During the fade-out, the piano switches over to the right in the stereo picture. Only during the "why why why" part, where McCartney's voice is treated with heavy echo, does his lead vocal appear in the right of the mix. An interesting side note to "Hello Goodbye": The band made a video of the song to send to Ed Sullivan for airing on his popular Sunday night variety show (mainly because they had quit touring by then and were not at all inclined to come to America to appear on a television show, yet still had the PR sensibilities to know they needed to promote their latest single). Here again, the Beatles were pioneering another form of media that we now take for granted: music videos. In the video, the band lip-synchs to the "Hello Goodbye" single, dressed in the uniforms they wore for the cover of *Sgt. Pepper*! Presumably, those uniforms should have been mothballed by the time they recorded "Hello Goodbye." Also, Lennon is seen playing an acoustic guitar, an instrument that does not appear on "Hello Goodbye."

"Strawberry Fields Forever": This was the first song recorded during the *Sgt. Pepper* sessions, so it makes sense that tape manipulation was front and center on it. Lennon's vocal sounds drunken and sloppy, such is the effect of his original vocal track being slowed down to fit the key in which they eventually recorded the song. Still, it works here, because it gives the song a necessary sadness and malaise. This track is loaded with instruments: The left channel is dominated by a Mellotron, drums, electric guitar, backward cymbals, backing vocals and a piano that doesn't make its appearance until the fade-out. The right includes another electric guitar, a keyboard that sounds like a celeste, bass, strings and horns. Lennon's double-tracked vocal appears squarely in the middle of the mix, where he also sings a brief harmony on the last chorus. The celeste and an acoustic guitar appear on the fade-out. The electric guitar on the right channel slides over to the left during the initial fade-out, and after the song comes back in, one can hear what sounds like a player piano—of all things—in the middle of the mix. Weird, guttural and extremely slowed down voicings can be heard on the left during the final fade-out.

"Penny Lane": McCartney's homage to boyhood memories has so many instruments and voices centered that at first listen, it sounds like a mono recording. The lead and backing vocals, piano, bass, drums, electric guitar and tambourine all appear in the center of the mix. A second piano, horns and the piccolo trumpet solo appear all the way right. During the choruses, the horns also appear on the left, along with bells. From 2:03 until 2:07, a cello appears on the left. The modulation to a higher key for the final chorus gives the song a joyous lift.

"Baby You're a Rich Man": A simple song with strange chord changes that features a wholly novel instrument, the Clavioline. It's a precursor of sorts to the Moog synthesizer that briefly enamored the rock cognoscenti during the late 1960s and early 1970s. The Clavioline part totally dominates this song, and is situated on the left channel, with an electric guitar. It has an Eastern sounding vibe to it, which fits in nicely with the Beatles' musical tendencies of the time. Piano, drums, maracas and a second electric guitar are all the way right, while Lennon's lead vocal (with occasional harmonies), McCartney's backing vocal, hand-claps and bass are centered. Listen for someone uttering an "oh oh" two seconds into the song.

"All You Need Is Love": An epic song, filled with a good vibe so befitting of the time it was recorded. Despite the iffy thesis (love probably isn't all you need), this song belongs in a time capsule as the perfect musical snapshot of 1967. The mix on this song would be completely redone for the 2009 remastered *Yellow Submarine* soundtrack album. On *Magical Mystery Tour*, however, "All You Need Is Love" gets the fake stereo treatment. Horns can be heard on both channels during the introduction, and then later in the song. The tremendously mournful backing vocals are all the way left, as are the handclaps that make their appearance at 2:57. The drum roll that accompanies the introduction is heard in the center, but during the rest of the song, the drums are panned to the right, where the horns, strings and piano can also be found. Listen for Paul McCartney saying "'kay" at exactly 24 seconds in. The bass, lead vocal, maracas and the electric guitar solo are all centered. Harrison's solo completely falls apart at 1:27. Lennon's lead vocal is double-tracked on the last two choruses and slides momentarily into the left of the stereo spectrum.

The Beatles (The White Album)

RELEASED NOVEMBER 22, 1968

"For the first time, I had to split myself in three ways because at any one time we were recording in different studios. You might have John in one studio and Paul in another with George and Ringo sort of going between them."

—*George Martin*[18]

"Well it is another step, you know, but it's not necessarily in the way people expected. On *Sgt. Pepper* we had more instrumentation than we'd ever had. More orchestral stuff than we'd ever used before, so it was more of a production. But we didn't really want to go overboard like that this time, and we've tried to play more like a band this time–only using instruments when we had to, instead of just using them for the fun of it."

—*Paul McCartney*[19]

The Beatles, more commonly known as *The White Album*, is an album full of musical contradictions and muscular songwriting. The band's first and only double album, it contains some of their best songs, and a few of their worst.

The album was released five years to the day after the release of their second album. The musical leaps and bounds the group had taken in five short years were astounding, and still represent the quickest maturation—in terms of ideas, innovation and cataclysmic creativity—of any rock band in the history of pop music.

Written and recorded after the band spent weeks (McCartney stayed for a month, Starr for only a few weeks; Harrison and Lennon stayed for roughly six weeks) in Rishikesh, India, studying at the feet of the Maharishi Mahesh Yogi, the album is flush with acoustic music, chiefly because they only had their acoustic guitars with them on their pilgrimage. Still, only three songs of the 30 here refer even remotely to their time in India.

Much has been made of the fact that *The White Album* is the album on which the fractures in the band became apparent, and that's certainly true, to an extent. Many of the songs were recorded without a full complement of the band on hand, and this is the point at which Yoko Ono made her presence in John Lennon's life known in no uncertain terms (much to the unbridled chagrin of the three other band members), yet I count 10 songs on which the full band absolutely makes the compelling case that they were the greatest rock quartet of all-time.

That said, it's clear that the writing team of Lennon-McCartney hadn't spent much time in the same room together in preparation for the album's recording. Out of the 30 songs here, only one ("Birthday") could reasonably be called a song-writing collaboration between the two.

The White Album contains both the Beatles' most whimsical songs ("The Continuing Story of Bungalow Bill," "Piggies" and "Rocky Raccoon") and also their scariest ("Helter Skelter," "Long Long Long" and "Revolution 9"). It's a neat summation of their range as songwriters and musicians.

The sheer breadth of the musical genres sampled on *The White Album* is astounding. From folk to acid rock, to Tin Pan Alley and ventures into the avante garde, it's all here. That they were able to pull it all off with a certain smug aplomb (and an obvious disconnect between the band members) makes this album an unmitigated triumph of style and taste. Throw in the fact that "Hey Jude" and the "fast" version of "Revolution" were recorded during the same sessions (but not included on the album), and you have ample evidence that *The White Album* was wildly productive and a wholly significant part of their entire output.

This is one of only two Beatles albums where it is necessary to harken back to the old days of vinyl record albums to fully understand the rationale behind the sequencing of the songs. Side one is bookended by two tremendous songs, with a lot of gimmicky filler tracks in between. Side two features four songs in which animals are the main characters, and a few more filler tracks. Side three is the one on which the band is playing together with noticeable skill and enthusiasm, and churning out some meaty rock and roll. Side four is a mishmash of rock music, a 1940s-style torch song, a weird, creepy sound collage of overwhelming insignificance, and a coda that would have made Mantovani proud.

By this time, Beatles' fans were pretty much disabused of the notion that the band would tour again anytime soon, and seemed content to wait out the gaps between studio releases to keep tabs on their heroes. The resounding success of *Sgt. Pepper* and the slightly lesser enthusiasm accorded to the disjointed *Magical Mystery Tour* only served to whet their appetite for more Beatles songs, and *The White Album* did not disappoint.

With only a handful of exceptions, the album is pretty much devoid of over-production and studio tricks designed to artificially sweeten the sound (unlike their previous two albums). *The White Album* contains music that is organic and simple, and therein lies its main appeal.

On headphones, the album sounds terrific. The handful of songs on which the acoustic guitar is the primary instrument have only a few interesting tidbits in the mix, but on the songs where the full band is playing, there are a lot of fascinating things to listen for.

John Lennon's songs are the strongest ones on *The White Album*. Clearly, he spent a lot of time playing his acoustic guitar in India, where he mastered a new picking technique that he used on both "Dear Prudence" and "Julia." His voice is raw and totally untouched by echo and reverb, a fact that gives his lyrics an extra dollop of meaning and gravity.

Paul McCartney seems to be practicing for his solo career. He plays drums on three songs, lead guitar on a couple of others, and five of his compositions here required no assistance from his bandmates. Still, he turns in two instant classics.

George Harrison contributes four songs to the album: Two of those songs ("While My Guitar Gently Weeps" and "Piggies") are considered to be among his best Beatles contributions, but the other two Harrison compositions are much more interesting songs (and recordings).

This is one of Ringo Starr's best albums in terms of his drumming, but he also wrote and sang the worst song on the album. He left the band for a time to work out some personal issues, but they continued to record in his absence. Still in all, his musical contributions are stellar.

"Back in the U.S.S.R.": The first sound one hears when listening to *The White Album* is the roar of a BOAC jet that moves across the stereo spectrum before the band comes in. McCartney plays drums, lead guitar and piano on this track, although some sources say the drum part is a patchwork affair cobbled together through the less-than-adequate drumming abilities of McCartney, Lennon and Harrison. This seems almost impossibly unlikely, as the Beatles at this point in their career would not have gone to all that trouble. One electric guitar, the drums and the backing vocals on the bridges are all the way left, while the lead guitar, piano and more drums reside on the right. McCartney's lead vocal (double-tracked in parts) is centered in the mix, where handclaps also appear during the guitar solo up through the end of the song. Legend has it that Lennon played the bass guitar, but I simply cannot discern a bass in this song.

"Dear Prudence": One of the best and most cerebral songs on the album starts out with two acoustic guitars on the right channel playing the sweet little intro, then at 16 seconds in, you can hear the engineer open the center track, where Lennon's doubled lead vocal and another acoustic guitar make their appearance. The drums, once again played by McCartney, are centered as well. On the left, one can hear the bass and backing vocals, a tambourine and two electric guitars during the middle eight. Handclaps appear left only during the final verse. The backing vocals during the middle eight also wander into the right channel briefly. The piano makes its first appearance at 3:02 into the song. Listen closely and you'll hear the fade-out eventually come to a cold end.

"Glass Onion": This tune references several Beatles songs by name, and also clues us in that the "walrus was Paul." A very simple mix includes bass and electric guitar on the left, drums, piano, tambourine and a recorder on the right. The snarling lead vocal, an acoustic guitar and some ominous sounding strings appear in the center.

Listen for someone to make a one-syllable high-pitched utterance at exactly 59 seconds into the song.

"Ob-La-Di, Ob-La-Da": The recording of this song went a long way toward exacerbating the band's foul mood when McCartney insisted they record it in a variety of tempos and styles. Lennon and Harrison didn't think the song was worthy of such a lengthy treatment, which totally tainted it forever in their minds. McCartney's lead vocals are heard on both the right and left channels, while the backing vocals are centered. Hand claps, bass, various percussion instruments and, on the last verse only, a second piano can be hard all the way left, while still more hand claps can be heard on the right. The main piano part, some horns and an acoustic guitar are centered in the mix. For a song that apparently fomented some bad feelings among the band, it nonetheless sounds like a fun recording, with Lennon and Harrison adding many colorful vocal adornments deep in the mix. Listen for Lennon to say "Home: H-O-M-E," starting at 2:14.

"Wild Honey Pie": This is all McCartney, producing an on-the-spot bit of whimsy that was tacked onto the album, presumably in an attempt to pad it. Not a thing appears in the center on the stereo picture, while an abundance of trebly acoustic guitars, vocals and percussion appear on the left and right.

"The Continuing Story of Bungalow Bill": A snippet of Spanish guitar, obviously cribbed from some stock recording, opens this adventurous tale of a big game hunter. A quick digression here: Lennon often said in interviews that he tried to always write about himself and wasn't interested in third-person "story" songs, a seemingly obvious swipe at McCartney, who did like to write those kinds of songs. Yet this is just one of many fictional character studies that Lennon wrote and recorded during his time with the Beatles ("Being for the Benefit of Mr. Kite," "Polythene Pam," "Mean Mr. Mustard" and others). The acoustic guitar, tambourine and backing vocals are on the left, and the drums, bass, more backing vocals and an organ appear on the right. The lead vocal and a weird sounding keyboard are centered. Occasionally, the lead vocal is doubled in the left channel. Listen for someone to say "Bill" 22 seconds into the song. Yoko warbles her one line at 1:46.

"While My Guitar Gently Weeps": This song, generally regarded as one of Harrison's masterpieces, is terribly overrated; it suffers from amateurish lyrics, a plodding tempo and a complete lack of the kind of musical twists and turns that often made the Beatles' music so interesting. The much-ballyhooed appearance of guest guitarist Eric Clapton only serves to drag the song down further. On the left one can hear piano and organ (both played by McCartney), Clapton's electric guitar (mixed way too high) and some percussion. The bass, drums and another electric guitar are on the right. Harrison's doubled lead vocal, with occasional harmonies from McCartney, are centered, along with a tambourine during the solo and the last part of the song. An acoustic guitar is also centered, but completely drops out from 1:53 until 1:58.

"Happiness Is a Warm Gun": The best song on the album has four distinct parts to it. Lennon's vocal goes from soothing to menacing in an instant, then eventually reverts to the soulful style he learned from listening to Stax and Motown records.

Lennon's lead vocal is tripled in parts, and shares the center of the stereo picture with an electric piano, electric guitar, and an acoustic piano during the last part of the song only. A bass guitar, electric guitar, tambourine and backing vocals are all the way left, where one can also hear someone "sing" a bass part during the last part of the song. The drums and another electric guitar are all the way right, where the lead vocal also appears at times. Listen for a stifled "eek" on the left channel at 1:34, and also for Lennon's falsetto reading of the word "gun" to appear faintly a millisecond before it actually climaxes the song at 2:21. McCartney and Harrison ably back up the lead singer with their "bang, bang, shoot shoot" rejoinders.

"Martha My Dear": Built around a very tricky piano part, and augmented by tasteful string and horn arrangements, this song is among McCartney's best on *The White Album*. His clear-eyed doubled lead vocal is centered in the mix, along with the drums, and an electric guitar and hand claps that both appear only during the middle eight. The piano and strings are left, with the horns and bass guitar appearing on the right. The bass plays the song out with five descending notes, which then turns into three ascending notes that introduce...

"I'm So Tired": Another superb Lennon composition, both in terms of melody and lyrics. The best part is that it's rendered so well; Lennon's vocal here is one of his finest ever. Both electric guitars are on the right, while the drums and bass appear on the left (although the drums occasionally leak into the center). Lennon's vocal is centered and fused with McCartney's harmony during the "little piece of mind" sections of the song. An organ can also be heard in the center of the mix.

"Blackbird": A simple yet elegant song, played in a style that caused budding acoustic guitarists the world over to try to figure out the odd two-note chording technique, along with the distinctive, pick-less plucking of the strings. McCartney's dry vocal is centered and doubled on the choruses only. His acoustic guitar (the peerless Martin D-28 model) is all the way to the right. Sounds of actual blackbirds chirping can be heard occasionally in the center of the mix. The percussive sound on the left is not, as many have posited, McCartney tapping his foot in time to the song: It's a pick hitting the pick-guard on his guitar, recorded on a separate track.

"Piggies": Harrison's denigration of the bourgeois is anchored by a harpsichord "borrowed" from another studio down the hall at Abbey Road. It and the lead and backing vocals are centered, while the bass, finger cymbals, strings and a tambourine are all the way left. On the right, one can hear an acoustic guitar, more strings and some unflattering barnyard sounds meant to make the point of the song even more obvious, as if that was necessary.

"Rocky Raccoon": McCartney's oater opus is introduced by the singer setting the stage in his best American West accent, accompanied only by a strident acoustic guitar that plays the same five chords (Am7, D7, G7, C, Em and back again) throughout the song, It's monotonous and totally without any salient point of view, but a fun little lark nonetheless. (The Beatles were chief purveyors of the notion that not every pop song needed to stir emotions or solve global problems.) The clean lead vocal is the only thing in the center of the mix, with the acoustic guitar, a harmonica, player piano and backing vocals all the way right. The drums and bass are on the left. Listen for the cymbals to make their appearance at 41 seconds in.

"Don't Pass Me By": While it's unfair to expect Ringo Starr to write masterpieces for the band, this might be the worst original Beatles song ever allowed a spot on one of their albums. Badly played, poorly written, and sung with a brio that belies the banality of the abysmal lyrics, it's puzzling why the group allowed this song to make the final cut. Starr's double-tracked vocal is the only thing in the center of the mix, while an organ and drums are on the left. The organ can also be heard on the right, with the bass and a countrified fiddle that completely overwhelms the song on the right. Listen for Starr to count from one to eight, starting at 2:38 in the right channel. The fade-out has a cold ending, a technique also employed on "Dear Prudence" and "Dr. Robert."

"Why Don't We Do It in the Road": Most Beatle histories have it that Starr played drums on this three-verse, four-in-the-bar pseudo-blues romp, but it sure sounds an awful lot like McCartney's drumming style. Although Ringo Starr has over the years claimed he was the drummer on this track, we know by now that the Beatles themselves are not the most reliable stewards of their own recording history. The drums here sound exactly like the drum parts McCartney played on his first solo album two years later. The drums introduce the song during the intro in the center, but move to the left, where the bass is also situated, for the rest of the song. The lead vocal, doubled in spots, is in the center, and the right features handclaps, piano and electric guitar. McCartney's rough-hewn vocal is in direct counterpoint to his vocals on the next song.

"I Will": This brief but heartfelt love song is McCartney plying the simple melodicism that would later become his signature songwriting motif. Sung in a sweet, if weary-sounding, vocal style, the tune is dominated by two expertly played acoustic guitars, one on the right, and the other centered, with occasionally forays into the left channel. Percussion, including wood blocks, can be found on the left channel, while an acoustic guitar and a "bass" part voiced by McCartney are on the right. McCartney harmonizes with himself during the middle eight. Harrison and Lennon do not appear on this track.

"Julia": There are nine songs on the second side of *The White Album*, but Lennon only contributed two. It's telling that his two are the best of the nine. "Julia" was the last song recorded for the album, and it's an achingly poignant ode to his mother, with peripheral references to Yoko Ono. Sung in a world-weary voice, the song is stark and simple. Over two acoustic guitars playing the exact same part (and employing the finger-picking technique he reportedly learned from Donovan in India), Lennon pulls off the melancholy inherent in the song's subject matter without seeming maudlin or coy. The guitars are centered and on the right (although the first guitar leaks into the left channel at times), and the vocal is doubled in spots.

"Birthday": A frenetic piece of stomp rock, "Birthday" is the only song on the album that appears to be a writing collaboration between Lennon and McCartney. The drums, two electric guitars, an organ, and a piano run through a speaker head all appear in the center of the mix. Lead vocals by Lennon and McCartney are doubled and appear in both the left and right channels, as do the occasional handclaps. The bass and a tambourine appear on the left, along with hopelessly breathless backing vocals supplied by Pattie Boyd and Yoko Ono that also leak into the right channel at times. Listen for McCartney to echo the guitar riff on his bass.

"Yer Blues": This is a fascinating song filled with sonic peccadilloes, and one that is unlike any other in the Beatles' canon. It's a straight blues screamer with well-placed stops and starts, before it morphs into a four-in-the-bar jam in which the entire band shows off their musical chops. An electric guitar and the main drum part are heard on the left, while two other electric guitars are on the right. Lennon's lead vocal, doubled at times, is centered, along with the bass. Listen for one of the microphones to feedback on the left channel at 1:20. Just as the band falls in for the instrumental break, a second drum part is introduced in the center at 2:24. Then, at 3:15, a rather sloppy edit returns the song to its original languorous tempo. Throughout the verse, another separate track with a Lennon vocal can be heard echoing the lines the main lead vocal has already delivered. It's a weird effect, and one that they emphasize in the fade-out, on which they have eliminated the main lead vocal entirely. McCartney's bass is as simple as it gets; he just plays the root notes throughout, without any of the typical fretboard oxbows, loops and swirls he usually employed.

"Mother Nature's Son": Only McCartney appears on this plaintive acoustic song based on the various lifts and hammers one can easily tap into when playing in the key of D major (Harrison used this technique on "Here Comes the Sun"). The acoustic guitar appears on the left (and gets noticeably louder 12 seconds into the song), while McCartney's lead vocal and some light percussion are centered. Understated horns are heard on the right, where one can also hear a light tapping sound 59 seconds into the song. Additional percussion during the instrumental break can be heard on the right, where a second acoustic guitar plays a counter-melody during the final portion of the song.

"Everybody's Got Something to Hide Except for Me and My Monkey": A fun little chunk of rock and roll that uses a clamorous cowbell, frantic handclaps, and much screaming and whooping to color the basic track. An electric guitar, cowbell, drums and a tremendously complex bass part can be heard on the left, with two additional crunchy guitars all the way right. During the drum break, the drums leach into the center of the mix and eventually all the way right. Lennon's doubled lead vocal is centered, along with most of the handclaps. I tried counting the number of "come ons" uttered in this song, but because Lennon triple-tracked them during the final instrumental break (and then added a few more during the fade-out) it was impossible to get a reliable count. Let's just say there are lots of them.

"Sexy Sadie": The bass guitar is the only thing that appears in the left channel, while an electric guitar and backing vocals appear on the right. A piano, treated with echo (which makes it sound slightly out of tune at times), Lennon's lead vocal, drums and a tambourine are in the center of the mix. A second electric guitar joins the fun during the lengthy fade-out, when Lennon vamps on some of the lines from the song. This is a soulful and dramatic deep album track, of the sort that most rock bands during this era would have given their eyeteeth to be able to write and record.

"Helter Skelter": Generally regarded as the most raucous Beatles song, "Helter Skelter" is acid rock at its most accessible. McCartney's spirited lead vocal—treated tastefully with just the right amount of reverb—appears in the center of the mix, along with an electric guitar and another guitar that plays the brief (and ham-fisted) solo. On the left are two more electric guitars and the bass. The drums and backing vocals appear on the right. An interesting note: The descending note walk-down on the electric guitar appears left on the first chorus, but is centered during the rest of the song. McCartney's lead vocal suddenly (and briefly) gets panned into the left channel at 1:13. The electric guitar in the center of the mix moves briefly to the left at 1:27. He plays the super-heavy bass part with a pick. Listen for Starr's famous "blisters" comment at 4:24.

"Long Long Long": This is one of the creepiest Beatle songs ever, with wistful lyrics, spare instrumentation and a spine-tingling close.

Harrison's vocal is triple tracked (one for each "long?"). The main acoustic guitar and the lead vocal are centered, with the two other harmony vocals appearing left and right. Bass, drums and a Mellotron are all the way left, with a second acoustic guitar and an organ appearing on the right. A piano appears centered in the mix during the middle eight only. The macabre fade to the song includes the sound of a creaking door and weird moaning sounds that mimic an ambulance siren.

"Revolution 1": The first song recorded for *The White Album* is a blues-rock treatment of the single "Revolution," which relied heavily on a thumping drum track and heavily distorted guitars for its signature sound. Here, an acoustic guitar leads things off, before two electric guitars make their appearance on the track. Lennon's doubled lead vocal, along with the generously layered backing vocals, are in the center of the mix, where one electric guitar and the acoustic guitar also reside. A piano makes its only appearance in the center of the mix by playing an arpeggio at 2:24. The other electric guitar, the bass and drums are all the way left. Horns can be heard on the right, but also on the left during the second verse only. Lennon's vocal on the fade-out goes from center to right to left, and then back again, as does one of the electric guitars.

"Honey Pie": McCartney's tribute to 1940s-era Hollywood torch songs gets the full band treatment. His pining lead vocal and the drums are centered, while an electric guitar and the piano are on the left. His vocal—complete with a scratchy megaphone effect—appears on the left from nine seconds in to the 16-second-mark. The jazzy electric guitar solo, expertly played by Lennon, appears on the right channel, where horns and various cymbal hits can also be found.

"Savoy Truffle": Harrison's paean to his (and Eric Clapton's) sweet tooth has a heavy horn arrangement that propels the song along with urgency. An electric piano, two electric guitars and an organ (during the last verse only) are centered, while the drums, some of the horns and another electric guitar are all the way left. Harrison's doubled lead vocal, bass and more horns are all the way right. Listen for a couple of surreptitious handclaps at 35 seconds in, and a high-pitched bird-like sound at 1:11 and then again a few measures later in the right channel, where the occasional sound of a tambourine can also be heard. Interestingly, the electric piano can only be heard during the introduction, and during the musical interlude before Harrison sings the second verse.

"Cry Baby Cry": Another Lennon story song, this one centered on numerous obscure Brit-centric references and a lead vocal mixed very low. The mix here is inventive; Lennon's lead vocal can be heard on the left during the intro and choruses only, before it reverts to the center for the verse. His occasional harmony vocal is also centered. The bass appears on the left channel, with the acoustic guitar and drums all the way right (except for some cymbal crashes that can also be heard on the left). An organ, piano, various sound effects and an electric guitar are centered. Listen for the electric guitar to get momentarily (and noticeably) louder at 1:25.

"Can You Take Me Back": A little acoustic-based song snippet from McCartney is included in the elapsed time of "Cry Baby Cry" and begins at 2:34. The acoustic guitar is on the right, percussion on the left and McCartney's high-pitched vocal in the center. Then, with 10 seconds remaining in the elapsed time of "Cry Baby Cry," an odd apology is given by someone to George Martin. Why they included this bit of weirdness begs reason.

"Revolution 9": There's really no point in parsing this overly long mishmash of tape loops, recorded conversation, scary sound effects and Yoko Ono's incoherent babbling. If you listen to it once on headphones, you won't ever need to listen to it again.

"Good Night": This beautiful lullaby is the perfect song to close an album so full of wildly eclectic musical styles, quirky songwriting and strange whimsy. Starr delivers the poignant vocals as only he could. Backed by a lavish string arrangement and a mixed chorus (that at times sings words that don't match what Starr is singing), Starr's lead vocal is centered, while the swelling strings appear on both the left and right channels. The chorus is centered, and a slightly audible piano can occasionally be heard on the left.

Yellow Submarine

RELEASED JANUARY 17, 1969

"Everything had to be tailor-made for the picture [*Yellow Submarine* film]. If a door opened or a funny face appeared at a window, and those moments needed to be pointed-up, it was the musical score that had to do the job. The answer is really very simple. You plan whatever tempo your rhythm is going to be, and then you lay down what is called a 'click track.' That is, a separate track, [that] simply contains a click sound which appears every so many frames of film. You know that 35-mm film runs at 24 frames per second, so knowing what tempo you want, you simply ask the film editor to put on a click at whatever interval you want. Then while conducting the orchestra, you wear headphones through which you can hear the clicks, and by keeping to that particular beat you 'lock in' the orchestra to the film. In that way you can write your score knowing that, even if something happens a third of the way or halfway through a bar, you can safely put in whatever musical effect you want, with absolute certainty that it will match the picture ... that is how I did it with 'Yellow Submarine.' I wrote very precisely even with avant-garde and weird sounds like 'Sea of Holes,' keeping to their bar-lines, knowing that the click track would ensure it fitted."

—*George Martin*[20]

The original 1969 release of *Yellow Submarine* contained six Beatles songs and six orchestral pieces composed by George Martin as incidental music for the film of the same name. The six Beatles songs included two that had been previously released ("Yellow Submarine" and "All You Need Is Love").

Other than the contribution of four new originals and a brief on-camera goof-off that appeared at the end of the movie, the Beatles themselves had very little to do with the making of the film. Actors were hired to voice the Beatles' parts, and the group played no role in scripting the film or sequencing the soundtrack.

The *Yellow Submarine* album was released twice again: The first time, in 1999, to correspond with the re-release of the film, and the final time as part of the 2009 release of the remastered Beatles catalogue.

The 1999 release did not include the George Martin compositions, but did include nine previously released Beatles songs that appeared in the original theatrical release. Best of all, the 1999 release was completely remixed, giving the songs a new lift and an astonishingly vibrant sonic quality. In some cases they sound like completely different songs.

For our purposes here, we will examine the original 1969 release (although not the Martin compositions, as they are not Beatles songs), and the 2009 release that incorporated the remix from the 1999 release and included a full remastering.

The 1969 release of *Yellow Submarine* is an odd assortment of weird songs that, in at least two cases, had been left over from previous recording sessions. A couple of them sound like they had been recorded during the *Sgt. Pepper* sessions, and the other two sound as if they would have fit in nicely on the *White Album*, which was released just two months prior to *Yellow Submarine*. Surprisingly, George Harrison was the composer of two of the four new songs on this album, while the two Lennon-McCartney compositions are quirky affairs that nonetheless deserve full marks for tunefulness and invention.

"Yellow Submarine": This includes the same exact mix and running time as the version that is on *Revolver*. Refer to that discussion for details.

"Only a Northern Song": This Harrison composition appears in the original release of the album as a mono version. Harrison himself plays organ, McCartney plays bass and an oddly clipped trumpet, Starr plays drums, and Lennon plays piano and a manic sounding glockenspiel part, of all things. At certain moments, a faint harmonica can be heard. Harrison's lead vocal is double-tracked. During the instrumental break and the longish fade-out, the voices of all four Beatles can be heard intoning indecipherable gibberish here and there.

"All Together Now": This song is two minutes and 10 seconds of studio tomfoolery of the sort that only the Beatles could pull off. Rather than it being a throw-away, gimmicky track, "All Together Now" is chock-full of savvy musicianship and a certain sing-along quality that they infused in even their most inconsequential songs. Two acoustic guitars, a ukulele, harmonica and a second lead vocal sung by McCartney can be found all the way left. The lead vocal is all the way right, with backing vocals on the line "look at me" only also all the way right. The bass, drums, finger cymbals and Lennon's double-tracked vocals on the bridges appear in the center of the mix. Handclaps abound, and various utterances, shouting and general vocal mayhem are woven throughout the mix. Listen for the tempo to really start speeding up at 1:27.

"Hey Bulldog": By far the most interesting of the songs here, "Hey Bulldog" finds the Beatles in rare form as a band, pulling out all the stops on a complicated but hooky 3:11 chunk of turbo-charged rock and roll. Because the piano and drums were recorded simultaneously on one track, and thus unable to be separated in the mix, they appear together all the way left. Only McCartney's bass guitar—stridently prominent on this track—appears in the middle during the verses. On the right channel, two electric guitars, the lead and backing vocals and some maracas can be heard. Lennon's double-tracked lead vocals appear in the middle of the mix during the middle eights, along with another drum part that is treated with some heavy reverb. Listen for Lennon and McCartney's human to canine "conversation" during the long fade-out on the right of the stereo spectrum.

"It's All Too Much": One of the biggest sounds the Beatles ever achieved in the studio, "It's All Too Much" is rife with distorted guitars that feed back, several different drum and percussive flavors, trumpets and a clarinet. In the left channel, a double-tracked lead vocal (which is also heard on the right channel) and various vigorous drum hits can be heard. The drums, an insistent cowbell, bass, organ and two electric guitars are centered in the mix. More drum hits, plus the clarinet and trumpets are all the way right in the mix. Maracas and a tambourine move in and out of the mix at various points in the track. McCartney sings a harmony vocal with Harrison on the last chorus and fade-out only, which can be heard in the left channel.

Listen for the sound of a ticking clock just before the song fades out completely.

"All You Need Is Love": This includes the same exact mix and running time as the version that is on *Magical Mystery Tour*. Refer to that discussion for details.

Yellow Submarine Soundtrack (2009 Remix)
Released September 13, 2009

The main difference between the 1969 release of *Yellow Submarine* and the 2009 remixed/remastered soundtrack is that the mixes are completely different and the sound is much louder. In some cases, the songs have slightly different running times. The 2009 version did not include the George Martin orchestral compositions, but added nine Beatles songs that had appeared on previous albums.

The remix turns these songs—all of them—on their head by giving them a newfound vibrancy and sheen that the original mixes didn't quite attain. It's difficult to argue that the original mixes didn't sound very good, but when juxtaposed against the remixed *Yellow Submarine*, they sound astonishingly limp and muddy. While everyone can agree that adding a touch of paint to a finished Picasso would be a terrible idea, one wonders what new sonic pleasures could be found in the entire Beatles catalogue if it was remixed in the same fashion.

"Yellow Submarine": On this version of the title song, all the instruments and Starr's lead vocal are centered, while the sounds of the sea wash from left to right in the stereo spectrum. The backing vocals and the background talk can be heard on both the left and right channels. During the last verse, when Lennon repeats the lines that Starr sings in his best cockney sea chantey voice, his words are treated with reverb and move slowly from right to left. Significantly, you can hear Lennon repeat "life of ease" here, whereas on the earlier version, that does not occur. The only other difference is the sound of a loud buzz for one second at 1:39.

"Hey Bulldog": This song is transformed by the remix. Instead of the lead and backing vocals being panned all the way right, here they appear in the center. The only thing that appears in the center in the original version is the bass guitar. On this version, the piano and drums are on the left, except for on the bridges, when the drums get centered and treated to reverb. Two electric guitars, bass, percussion and lots of shouting during the solo appear on the right. The electric guitar solo is double-tracked. Listen to a stray bark at 1:32, following immediately by Lennon saying "yeah."

"Eleanor Rigby": The version of this song on *Revolver* has McCartney's lead vocal all the way right, with the strings centered and the backing vocals on the left. On this version, the lead vocals are centered, with the violin and viola on the left, and the cellos on the right. Also, the vocals are brought way up in the mix. This version is two seconds shorter in elapsed time, probably due to a minor variance in tape speed. "Eleanor Rigby" is a much better sounding song on this album.

"Love You To": The mix for this song is generally the same as the version on *Revolver*, except that everything is louder, and this version is faded out three seconds sooner than the original.

"All Together Now": The main difference here is that the backing vocals appear on both channels, and the lead vocal is centered rather than panned right. Also, the drums are panned right here, whereas previously they appeared centered in the mix. The acoustic guitar, ukulele, harmonica and a second lead vocal remain on the left channel.

"Lucy in the Sky with Diamonds": Here, the bass, drums, double-tracked lead vocal and backing vocals are all centered. An electric guitar and organ can be heard on the right. The Mellotron is on the left, and you can hear a faint acoustic guitar, also on the left, that you can't hear on the original. The significant difference on this version is that the drums sound like they are playing a completely different part, and are brought way up in the mix.

"Think for Yourself": There is one main difference between this version and the one on *Rubber Soul*: Here, the lead vocal is double-tracked and centered, where on the previous version two lead vocals appeared on the left and the right.

"Sgt. Pepper's Lonely Hearts Club Band": This song was immediately improved by the centering of McCartney's lead vocal, which had been shoved all the way to the right on the previous version. The crowd noises appear in the center during the introduction, before moving to the left, and veering to the right during the last verse only. Backing vocals appear in both channels, while one electric guitar is on the right, and the horns are all the way to the left. The bass, drums and a second electric guitar are centered.

"With a Little Help from My Friends": The remix moves the piano from center to the left, and the electric guitar from center to the right. The backing vocals appear on both channels here. The "questions" posed by Lennon and McCartney are left and right on the last verse only. Also, the electric guitar part is louder and can be heard more easily in this mix. Listen for a guttural one-syllable utterance at 2:28.

"Baby You're a Rich Man": The main differences in this mix include the centering of the drums and bass, leaving only the piano on the right channel (although slight intimations of a second electric guitar can occasionally be heard there). The Clavioline and the lead guitar remain all the way left.

"Only a Northern Song": This is the first appearance of the stereo version of "Only a Northern Song." Consequently, it sounds fuller and richer. The organ part, played by Harrison, appears intermittently on both channels. A piano and some percussion appear on the right. Harrison's double-tracked lead vocal is centered, but also veers left at times.

The bass and drums remain centered, where you can also hear the occasional clumsy trumpet toots, played by McCartney. Harrison harmonizes with himself only on a single word ("brown") at 1:42.

"All You Need is Love": Other than "Hey Bulldog," this is the song most improved by the remix. The muddiness evident on the *Magical Mystery Tour* and original *Yellow Submarine* versions is completely remedied by the remix. Here, the song is slowed down a bit, and fades out more rapidly; this version is five seconds shorter. Lennon's lead vocal has been treated with some reverb. Most of the instruments appear in their original locations in the mix, except the horns also appear in the center of the mix on this version. Moreover, the drums are centered in the mix and the bass is louder. The backing vocals appear on both channels, as does the piano. But the most significant difference is that the strings are pulled way up in the mix, making them louder and more dramatic. Once again, the harmonies change completely during the final chorus. The handclaps on the fade-out are louder and appear on both channels.

"When I'm Sixty-Four": Here, the lead vocal is centered and clearer. The bass and drums are also centered. The oboes and clarinet still reside on the right, with the chimes remaining on the left. Another big difference is that the backing vocals are centered instead of on the right, where they were on the original version.

"Nowhere Man": First, and most importantly, the remixed "Nowhere Man" is stripped of almost all of the overbearing reverb that could be heard on the original mix. On the *Rubber Soul* version, there is virtually nothing in the center of the stereo picture; all the vocals are all the way right, while all of the instruments (except for the guitar solo) are all the way left. On the remix, the acoustic guitar, drums and bass are all centered, while the doubled lead vocal can be heard on both channels, as can the backing vocals. The electric guitar and electric guitar solo are panned all the way right.

"It's All Too Much": The chief differences on the remix of "It's All Too Much" are that the horns appear on both channels, the feedback on the guitars is more prominent, and the organ, treated with some echo, appears left rather than in the center. Also, Harrison's lead vocal is brought up in the mix. Overall, the remix gives this song a bigger sound. It's transformed into 6:25 of proto-acid rock.

Abbey Road

RELEASED SEPTEMBER 27, 1969

"During the album things got a bit more positive and, although it had some overdubs, we got to play the whole medley. We put them in order, played the backing track and recorded it all in one take, going from one arrangement to the next. We did actually perform more like musicians again. Likewise with the vocal tracks: we had to rehearse a lot of harmonies and learn all the back-up parts. Some songs are good with just one voice and then harmonies coming in at different places and sometimes three-part work. It's just embellishment, really, and I suppose we made up parts where we thought it fitted because we were all trying to be singers then."

—George Harrison [21]

"For the first time we were using a transistorized mixing console. Up to this point, all the albums had been recorded on a tube desk. But this luxurious transistorized desk had a limiter and compressor on every channel and selectable frequencies—it was quite a change. Regarding Ringo's drums, this was the first time I was able to record his kit in stereo because we were using eight-track instead of four-track. Because of this, I had more mic inputs, so I could mic from underneath the toms, place more mics around the kit—the sound of his drums were finally captured in full. I think when he heard this he kind of perked up and played more forcefully on the toms, and with more creativity."

—Geoff Emerick [22]

"After the *Let It Be* nightmare, *Abbey Road* turned out fine. The second side is brilliant. Out of the ashes of all that madness, that last section is for me one of the finest pieces we put together."

—Ringo Starr [23]

"To me, listening to *Abbey Road* is like listening to somebody else. It doesn't feel like the Beatles, but overall I think it's a very good album."

—George Harrison [24]

Abbey Road was the last Beatles album recorded by the group, although it was released before *Let It Be*. It's by far the finest Beatles album from their late period, and stands as one of the best final albums ever recorded by a rock group.

It's impossible to parse this album without reverting to an old school discussion of the two "sides" of the album, as they appeared on vinyl in their original form. Side one is a collection of complete songs that gave each member of the group a chance to show off his songwriting chops circa 1969 (two Lennon songs, two by McCartney, and one each by Harrison and Starr). Side two includes three complete songs, a suite of magnificent music deftly melded together (with an astounding climax), and an off-the-cuff lark that seeks to defuse the gravitas of the preceding 16-plus minutes. Both sides' final songs end abruptly, before their final notes are played.

Abbey Road is a musical accomplishment of epic span, and features some of the best singing, playing and songwriting of the group's entire career. It is also the most polished album they ever released, with production values that created the studio blueprint for the coming decade.

It is by far the most interesting Beatles album to listen to on headphones. It's full of stereo eccentricities, wild panning and in-your-face instrumentation. Just when you think you've identified each guitar part on a particular track, a new one is introduced into the mix.

The band decided to wash away the sour memory of the *Let It Be* sessions by getting back into the studio and making an album the way in which they had become accustomed: Laying down a basic track, and then layering that with additional instruments and vocals until they had a finished product. This album is filled with overdubs, but uses very few vocal sweetening effects, like echo, reverb or chorus.

There is very little in the way of songwriting collaboration on this album. The only song here that can in any way be called a collaboration is Starr's "Octopus's Garden," on which he had ample help from Harrison. All the rest of the songs were written entirely by the lead singer.

The Beatles, like many other bands in 1969, had a brief but fervent infatuation with the Moog synthesizer, an outsized contraption that could make all manner of unusual noises, musical or otherwise. They used a Moog on at least four songs on *Abbey Road*.

This is the only Beatles album not to have the band's name printed on its cover. It remains the best-selling Beatles studio album of all-time.

John Lennon turns in an interesting set of songs. Two are full-out blues-inflected rock numbers with great guitars, one is a hypnotic existential musing with gorgeous harmonies layered over lots of minor and diminished chords, and the rest are broken fragments of full songs, infused with a dab of the old Lennon whimsy.

McCartney's main contributions include the suite of melodic song snippets that bring the album to a dramatic close, and unparalleled bass playing throughout. He also seems to have almost completely taken over the keyboard chores for the band; his piano and electric piano work can be heard on almost every song on the album.

Abbey Road contains Harrison's two best compositions, with the Beatles and beyond. His singing is as good as it ever was (or ever would be), and both his electric and acoustic guitar playing is superlative here. Harrison's guitar playing is soulful and heartfelt. Just listen to the brief solo he plays on "Carry That Weight" (starting at 35 seconds into the song). It's one of the defining moments on this album. He also contributes some Moog noodling to a couple of songs.

This is one of Starr's two finest albums on drums, along with *Sgt. Pepper*. The tasty fills and inventive use of the floor bass drum and tom toms make the sound of the songs fuller. He also contributes his first and only drum solo on a Beatles record. Plus, he weighs in with his finest composition as a Beatle.

"Come Together": Around a snaky rhythm track of drums, bass and electric guitar, Lennon weaves his characteristic wordplay into the mix. The lead vocal, harmony vocal and bass appear in the center of the mix. The electric guitar solo is also centered, where maracas can also be heard on the outro only. The rhythm guitar is on the left and the drums and electric piano appear on the right. Listen for some vigorous background shouting right after the instrumental break at 2:30. This is one of the only Beatles songs on which Lennon and McCartney sing harmony, with McCartney taking the lower part.

"Something": Easily the most polished song on the album, the musical execution on "Something" is nearly flawless. The organ and rhythm guitar are on the left, with the very energetic bass part taking up the entire right channel. The drums, lead guitar solo and lead vocal are centered. There are some strings in the center as well. A piano appears during the middle eight only. McCartney sings harmony with Harrison on the middle eight, and Harrison doubles his vocal on the last verse.

"Maxwell's Silver Hammer": It's unfortunate that such a fine album as *Abbey Road* includes one of the Beatles' worst songs ever, but it does, and here it is. It's easy to see why the other Beatles objected to McCartney's pointless little serial killer melodrama (delivered in such a cheery manner, with lots of vocal winks and nudges): There is so much instrumentation on this song that one can only imagine the work it took to put it together. The piano, bass and a Moog appear left, with drums and another moog part on the right. The center of the mix is so laden with stuff that it's hard to distinguish what's what. The lead and backing vocals, two electric guitars, acoustic guitar, yet another moog part and the banging of a metal anvil all muddy up the center of the mix. The acoustic guitar appears only on the second and third choruses, and one line of backing vocals can be heard on the left during the third verse.

"Oh! Darling": McCartney quickly redeems himself with this old-time rocker, complete with 1950s-style chord changes and a vocal that would seem daunting to a lesser talent. Only the piano appears in the left channel, and only the stabbing electric guitar appears on the right (listen for the broken stroke on the guitar at 1:07). McCartney's inspired lead vocal and bass, plus the drums and backing vocals appear in the center. The backing vocals are doused in reverb, and for a split second there is some echo applied to McCartney's vocal (at 1:41). The backing vocals come in at different points in each verse, and turn "Oh! Darling" into a sonic delight. This is one of the finest Beatles songs that wasn't a hit.

"Octopus's Garden": Starr's best original has the entire band making key contributions. Lennon's picked electric rhythm guitar part, Harrison's electric guitar solo, McCartney's piano and bass, and outstanding backing vocals by Lennon and McCartney turn this into a true band effort. The backing vocals appear on both channels, while the lead vocal, bass, Harrison's guitar and the main piano part are centered. Lennon's electric guitar is all the way left, while the drums and another piano, playing only the bass notes, appear on the right. Starr's second vocal, designed to augment the lead vocal, appears sporadically on the right. The "aahs" sung by McCartney during the electric guitar solo are put through a processor to make it sound like he's under water, and travel from left to right and then back again in the stereo spectrum. One thing that distinguishes this track is the outstanding backing vocals by Lennon and McCartney, pushed way high up in the mix. They sound as good as ever singing together here, and put the lie to the often advanced notion that internal rifts had forever damaged their ability to sound like the two fresh faced lads from Liverpool who spent their formative years developing the vocal harmony sound that was the hallmark of their earliest hits. That they delivered such a great performance on a Ringo Starr song demonstrates that they were, at least on some level, still very interested in being the Beatles.

"I Want You (She's So Heavy)": No other Beatles song sounds even remotely like "I Want You." Based on a bluesy guitar riff and backed by bass, organ and drums, it goes on a seven-minute-forty-seven-second odyssey before abruptly ending right in the middle of the sixteenth repeat of the play-out chord sequence. The third verse is played slightly faster and has some jazzy undertones to it. The drums and one electric guitar are on the left, while the organ is on the right (although during the play-out jam, another electric guitar can be heard on the right). The lead vocal, backing vocals, lead electric guitar and bass are centered in the mix, as is the white noise generator, first heard at 5:42 (and which gets progressively louder and begins to overwhelm the song before it ends). Listen to the incredible bass runs that McCartney plays, starting at 4:04.

"Here Comes the Sun": Built around a D major chord, this song retains it's sunny feel throughout, even during the middle eight that is played in a completely different key. Harrison's lead vocal starts out in the center, but is moved right during the second verse, and stays there for the rest of the song. The main acoustic guitar, plus the bass and drums are centered. Harmony vocals, sung by Harrison and McCartney (Lennon does not appear on this track), appear on the right, along with a Mellotron. A second acoustic guitar, moog and organ are on the left. Handclaps can be heard, starting at 1:50, and move left to right and back again, as does one of the acoustic guitars, until every instrument takes its original place in the stereo picture for the last verse. George Harrison never sounded so good.

"Because": What's so interesting about this recording is how the Beatles' harmonies had matured since they sang the exultant chorus to "She Loves You" six years earlier. The block harmonies on that tune were as inventive as anything recorded during the early 1960s, and the world-weary but complicated and precise harmonies on "Because" are just as ground breaking. The voices sound older, for sure, but they also somehow sound wiser and more in command. As the 1960s were about to move aside for the new decade, the Beatles were still setting the musical pace. Lennon, McCartney and Harrison recorded their three-part harmony three times over to give this song the definitive vocal swell it's known for. A harpsichord plays the first few chords on the left, and is echoed by an electric guitar (playing the same exact part throughout), beginning 12 seconds into the song. The simple bass part is centered. Listen for the moog to play a countermelody beginning at 1:30. Ending this song on a diminished chord was a stroke of genius.

"You Never Give Me Your Money": This is by far the most complicated recording and mix on the album. The song is comprised of four distinct parts, and is somehow perfectly woven together in just over four minutes. A plaintive piano begins the tune, over which two electric guitars (one left and one right) are layered. McCartney's doubled lead vocal is centered, but moves to the right in the mix over the barrelhouse piano that dominates the second part of the song. The bass is centered, as is still another electric guitar during the third part of the song. McCartney sings a harmony vocal over his lead vocal, which is briefly treated with heavy reverb at 1:05. A tambourine can be heard on the fade-out only. A synthesizer can also be heard at times in the center of the mix. During the repeated recitation of the children's incantation during the fade-out, the backing vocals move from the center, to the left, to the right, and then back again. Then, the sound of crickets and chimes can be heard as they usher in the next track.

"Sun King": If it's possible, this song is even sleepier than "I'm So Tired" and "I'm Only Sleeping." With harmonies that sound very much like those in "Because," the song meanders along over a heavily phased guitar that moves throughout the track from left to right and back again. A second electric guitar introduces each measure with a simple five-note figure, and is centered, along with the lead and harmony vocals. Some cymbals introduce the song on the left, but the drums are all the way right in the mix, where an organ part is also situated. A bass is on the left, along with some of the vocals, and some percussion and maracas can be heard toward the end of the song.

"Mean Mister Mustard": A very simple mix is featured on this brief tune with an oddly syncopated time signature. The lead and harmony vocals are centered, while the drums and an electric guitar are on the right. A synthesizer and tambourine appear on the left, along with one of the harmony vocals on the second verse only. The tambourine drops in and out of the mix throughout the song.

"Polythene Pam": The next two songs in the suite were recorded live in the studio, with vocals and various overdubs added later. Here, the acoustic guitar that introduces the song appears in the center, but is quickly moved to the left when the vocals start. The lead and backing vocals and bass are centered, while an electric guitar and maracas are on the right. There is a lot of studio chatter heard on the left channel during the guitar solo, and yet another electric guitar is added to the left in the mix during the segue into the next song.

"She Came in Through the Bathroom Window": McCartney's doubled lead vocal is centered, along with his bass, while the electric guitar and drums are on the right. An acoustic guitar, backing vocals, tambourine and some added incidental percussion (during the second verse only) are all on the left.

"Golden Slumbers": An elegantly simple and beautiful song, sung with clear-eyed emotion, "Golden Slumbers" kicks off the scintillating three-song coda to the album. The piano is centered during the introduction only, then moves right, where the horns will eventually be heard. The lead vocal, bass, drums and strings are all the way left in the mix. Harrison plays the bass on this track. As you listen to this track, try to isolate the strings and horns on the last two lines. This is the signature sound of the Beatles, ably assisted by the incomparable talents of George Martin.

"Carry That Weight": The drums, bass and strings appear on the left, with a second drum part, piano and horns on the right. This leaves the center of the mix for the lead vocals, the brief but effective guitar solo, and a second electric guitar that plays out the song right into the next track. McCartney reprises "You Never Give Me Your Money" here, and harmonizes with himself on that part of the song. The choruses are sung with gusto by all four Beatles, making this only the third time that all four sang together on a Beatles song ("Yellow Submarine" and "Flying" being the other two).

"The End": The drums were double-miked, allowing them to be placed in the left, center and right of the mix here. The brief lead vocal that comes just before the guitar jam is also centered. The drum solo bounces all over the stereo picture, until the electric guitars, bass and drums appear in the left channel. At this point, you get to hear—one last time—the amazing rhythm section of McCartney and Starr on bass and drums laying down the foundation of an epic jam, which is then augmented by two electric guitars, played by Lennon and Harrison, playing the same two chords (A7 and D7) over and over again. The "love yous" voiced by Lennon, McCartney and Harrison, start on the right but move to the left just before the three trade guitar solos. McCartney goes first, with Harrison and Lennon following. All the guitar solos are in the center of the mix. It all comes to an abrupt halt, at which point a lone piano can be heard playing a single three-finger chord. McCartney's vocal returns and delivers the final proclamation from the group, over a swell of piano, strings, drums, bass, harmony vocals and two electric guitars.

"Her Majesty": This musical postscript crashes in with the unused ending of "Mean Mr. Mustard." ("Her Majesty" was originally slated to appear between "Mean Mr. Mustard" and "Polythene Pam" in the suite.) Over an urgently picked acoustic guitar, McCartney offers his little love note to the Queen. The acoustic guitar and vocal start out all the way right, but end up all the way left by the time the song ends in just 23 seconds.

Let It Be

Released May 8, 1970

"I'm not really interested in the production of our records. In fact, I wish I didn't have to go through that whole thing, going through the production and balancing the bass and all that. For me, the satisfaction of writing a song is in the performing of it. The production bit is a bore. If some guy would invent a robot to do it, then it would be great. But all that 'get the bass right, get the drums right,' that's a drag to me. All I want to do is get my guitar out and sing songs."

—John Lennon [25]

"It was always understood that the album would be like nothing the Beatles had done before. It would be honest, no overdubbing, no editing, truly live … almost amateurish. When John brought in Phil Spector he contradicted everything he had said before. When I heard the final sounds I was shaken. They were so uncharacteristic of the clean sounds the Beatles had always used. At the time Spector was John's buddy, mate and pal.... I was astonished because I knew Paul would never have agreed to it. In fact I contacted him and he said nobody was more surprised than he was."

—*George Martin*[26]

"I think the original idea was Paul's—to rehearse some new songs, pick a location and record the album of the songs in a concert. We would learn the tunes and record them without loads of overdubs."

—*George Harrison*[27]

Although *Let It Be* was recorded before *Abbey Road,* it was released eight months after, leading some critics to advance the unfounded argument that the band wrapped their recording career on somewhat of a down note.

The recording of *Let It Be* has become the standard-bearing joke about a rock and roll band in disarray, fighting with each other and looking and sounding wholly disinterested in working together. Much has been written about the terrible time the Beatles had in the studio recording the album, and many rock critics gave the album less than enthusiastic marks at the time of its release (chiefly because they seemed to buy into the notion that internal disharmony supposedly pervaded the project).

And, it is true that the January 1969 recording sessions in Twickenham Studios were not swathed in the warm glow of friendship and love. The Beatles initially undertook the project with the notion that the sessions would be filmed so fans could get a glimpse of "the Beatles at work on their new album." Then, the defining moment of the proposed film would be the first Beatles' live performance since 1966. Both were excellent ideas, and typically innovative for the time.

They just couldn't quite pull it off. Marred by varying degrees of disinterest, burgeoning use of dangerous pharmaceuticals, dissatisfaction among some band members who were being instructed how and what to play, disagreement as to who should produce and mix the album, and a generally negative atmosphere, the ambitions for the project were scaled back considerably.

All of this aside, *Let It Be* has actually aged better than many of the band's albums. It has several really fine songs on it, and a listen by the uninitiated betrays no obvious bad vibes between the band members.

In the end, the main issue was the production. George Martin produced the uninspired January sessions, which were then handed over to Glyn Johns to mix. Lennon and Harrison didn't like the finished product, and gave the master tapes to Phil Spector, who promptly lathered up the songs with a froth of indulgent overproduction that included cloying string arrangements and worse, an angelic chorus that sounded like what might greet you at the gates of St. Peter. This is the version that was released, much to the dismay of Paul McCartney, who wanted to cleave to the original idea of a Beatles album with bare bones production values.

McCartney would get his wish 33 years later, when he would be the chief moving force behind the release of *Let It Be ... Naked*, a re-release of the album stripped bare of the onerous wall of sound treatment. That album also eliminated the witty repartee before and after some of the songs, and completely reworked the running order. (A discussion of *Let It Be ... Naked* follows the present chapter.)

The Beatles quickly set about to burnish their reputation by regrouping in the studio during the summer of 1969 to record *Abbey Road*, by every measure a more polished and more impressive sounding album.

Still, *Let it Be* sounds much better today when it's taken out of its original context in the Beatles catalogue. It contains lots of hooky songs, with tasty guitars, and organs and electric pianos played by Billy Preston (the first and only time the band allowed someone else to participate in the recording of an entire album). It also is notable for the almost complete lack of all three of the band's vocalists singing at the same time, a technique they used on most of their albums.

Lennon contributes only three full songs to the album, but unlike on *The White Album,* he can be heard on most of the songs here. His guitar is prominent throughout, and he adds some rich harmonies to some of McCartney's compositions.

McCartney dominates the proceedings, and offers up three songs that are considered Beatles classics. Unlike the previous five albums, his bass playing is not nearly as inventive or prominent on *Let It Be.*

Harrison weighs in with two songs, both imbued with an uncharacteristic sense of humor. His guitar playing is stellar throughout.

Starr vacillates between all-out drum bashing and playing understated parts designed to subtly underscore the drama of the song. As usual, whatever is called for in the particular song, Starr delivers.

One additional note: This album includes virtually no handclaps, maracas, tambourine or other percussive instruments, a marked departure from most Beatles albums. This is likely a result of the fact that many of the songs were recorded live and not treated to heavy overdubbing. Only two songs here feature any added percussion instruments.

"Two of Us": Lennon and McCartney teamed up for this simple folk song with easy harmonies, based around a playful acoustic guitar interplay. One guitar is panned left, the other right. The center features both vocals, drums and an electric guitar sitting in for the absent bass. The song is faded naturally, with the acoustic guitars playing more softly until they can't be heard at all. The electric guitar, strangely, does not fade. McCartney bids the listener farewell over Lennon's whistling.

"Dig a Pony": Another Lennon song limned with odd lyrics, but rendered enthusiastically by the entire band. The drums, bass and electric piano can be heard in the center of the mix, while two crunchy electric guitars can be heard, one on the left and the other on the right. The lead and harmony vocals are situated between the center and the left in the mix.

"Across the Universe": This is one of at least three recorded versions of this beautiful song, which includes lyrics that are among Lennon's best. The song was written in 1967. Lennon sings the heartfelt lyrics over a single plaintive acoustic guitar, all centered in the mix, where maracas and an electric guitar with a wah-wah effect can also be heard. The left and right channels are overrun by strings and a mixed chorus, which totally overwhelms the song at times.

"I Me Mine": This is the only Beatles song that was partially recorded in 1970, making it, obviously, the last Beatles song to be recorded. Harrison's waltzy verses slowly turn into a four-in-the-bar rock and roll extravaganza, and then back again. The drums, bass, lead and harmony vocals are centered. An electric guitar, organ and horns are on the left, while another electric guitar, acoustic guitar and strings can be heard on the right. Harrison's lead vocal is doubled on the last line only. Lennon does not appear on this track.

"Dig It": This in-studio jam apparently went on for more than 10 minutes, but luckily the Beatles saw fit to only include a snippet of it here. The piano is on the left, an organ and an electric guitar are on the right, with Lennon's vocal and the drums centered. Once again, there is no bass on this track. A few electric guitar notes can be heard on the left under McCartney's shrill introduction of the next tune.

"Let It Be": McCartney's pass at writing a gospel song with rock and roll sensibilities, the version here is the best of the three the band recorded, mainly because of the searing guitar solo played by Harrison. The lead vocal, piano, drums, bass and electric piano are all in the center of the mix, and the solo is centered as well. Maracas can be heard on the last verse only. Horns and the backing vocals (treated with slight reverb) can be heard in both the left and right channels. An organ can be heard on the right.

"Maggie Mae": A few seconds of an old Liverpool folk song takes the serious quotient back down several notches. Lennon's heavy Scouse-inflected lead vocal is on the left, over his acoustic guitar. McCartney's harmony vocal—slipping off-key at times—is on the right, over his acoustic guitar. An electric guitar and drums can be heard in the center of the mix.

"I've Got a Feeling": One of the most interesting songs on the album to listen to on headphones, "I've Got a Feeling" is an old school singing collaboration between Lennon and McCartney. Over two electric guitars (one left and one right) McCartney sings the verses and middle eight, with his voice centered (and with an occasional overdubbed harmony vocal). An electric piano can be heard on the left. The drums and bass are in the center, where Lennon's vocal also appears. On the last verse, McCartney's vocal is on the left, while Lennon delivers his part all the way right. This makes for a very interesting mix.

"One After 909": Lennon resurrected this song, originally written in 1962, and ramped up its rock and roll urgency with the raucous and deliciously loose version heard here. It has the simplest mix on the album: The lead and harmony vocals, bass and drums are centered, while one electric guitar and the electric piano can be heard on the left. Another electric guitar is on the right.

"The Long and Winding Road": This is the most contentious track on the album, chiefly because McCartney objected to the sonic goo that Spector slathered all over it. The overbearing string arrangement is on the left, and the horns are all the way right. The center contains the lead vocal (at times completely swallowed up by the overproduction), piano, bass (played by Lennon), and the female chorus. A barely audible electric guitar can be heard at times between the left and the center in the mix.

"For You Blue": Harrison's fun little four-bar blues has the band playing in complete harmony with each other. The lead vocal, acoustic guitar and drums are centered, while Lennon's slide guitar and a bass are on the left. The most interesting sound comes from the piano in the right channel. Tacks were inserted into the felt surfaces of the piano's hammers on the right side of the keyboard, giving the notes played there a ticky-tack quality, while the left side of the keyboard is not affected likewise.

"Get Back": Again, there were several versions of this song recorded, some with additional verses and different mixes. McCartney's simple bass part and Starr's galloping drums are centered, where the lead and harmony vocals also reside. Preston's signature electric piano solo is also centered. Lennon's lead guitar can be heard on the left, while Harrison's spare, staccato electric guitar strokes can be heard on the right. This is the sound of a band definitely "passing the audition."

Let It Be ... Naked
RELEASED NOVEMBER 17, 2003

Let It Be ... Naked purports to be the album the Beatles originally set out to make when they convened for the sessions for *Let It Be.*

By the time of its release, John Lennon and George Harrison were dead, calling into question whether they would have approved of this reworking of one of their original albums. Apparently, Ringo Starr gave the project his blessing, but make no mistake about it, this album exists because of Paul McCartney's simmering and long-standing animus toward those he held responsible (Lennon, Phil Spector, Allen Klein) for the sonic quality of the original version.

Let It Be ... Naked has a completely different running order: "Dig It" and "Maggie Mae" were eliminated, and "Don't Let Me Down" was added to the set. Most prominently, the songs were stripped of the strings, horns and choruses that added a saccharine quality, particularly to songs like "Let It Be," "The Long and Winding Road" and "Across the Universe."

Some of the songs here have completely different mixes, and several of them have different vocals. A couple of the tracks sound pretty much the same as the *Let It Be* versions.

Let It Be ... Naked also came with a bonus disc called *Fly on the Wall*, consisting of 21:55 of out-takes, impromptu jams and barely discernible chatter. Listening to it a single time will probably be enough for even diehard Beatles fans.

This album has been completely stripped of the studio chatter before and after songs that gave *Let It Be* a large part of its personality. In its place are cold starts and ends to most of the songs. Even some of the in-song chatter has been eliminated.

"Get Back": This track has the same mix, but is missing the tuning and chatter that precedes the original, and the "hope we passed the audition" remark that closes the original album.

"Dig a Pony": This track has the same mix as well, but does not include the pre- and post-song banter.

"For You Blue": On this version, the piano is on the left and the slide guitar is on the right, opposite of the original mix. The bass has also been repositioned from the left to the center, where the acoustic guitar, lead vocal and drums also reside. The acoustic guitar is much more prominent in this mix.

"The Long and Winding Road": Paul McCartney was wrong; this stripped down version is inferior to the strings and chorus laden version on the original album. As lamentable as the overwrought production on the original was, the vocal is better and it's a more dramatic sounding piano ballad. This version sounds like a demo tape. The piano, vocal, bass and drums are centered, while an electric piano takes the place of the strings on the left, and an organ and electric guitar replace the horns on the right. The vocal on this version is completely different, and not nearly as effective as the original. For the definitive version of "The Long and Winding Road" as McCartney probably intended it to sound, listen to the version on the 1977 live album *Wings Over America*.

"Two of Us": This mix is exactly the same, except for the elimination of the spoken intro, and a quicker fade-out.

"I've Got a Feeling": This mix is much different than the original, in almost every way. The reverb has been removed from McCartney's lead vocal, and the sound on the electric guitars has been cleaned up a bit. McCartney's vocal is completely different, and much stronger here.

Unlike the original version, the mix keeps McCartney and Lennon's vocals during the last version centered, rather than panning them to opposite channels. The drums and bass remain centered, and the electric piano is moved from the left to the center.

"One After 909": Other than the guitars being treated with heavy compression here, this mix is exactly the same as the original. This mix also reduces some of McCartney's vocal asides, and features a cold finish without the studio chatter.

"Don't Let Me Down": Lennon's bluesy tribute to Yoko Ono finds the band playing in perfect harmony with each other. Unfortunately, the single version that is on *Past Masters Two* is far superior to this version. This version is played much faster and the vocals aren't nearly as plaintive and dramatic. The electric piano is on the left, while one of the electric guitars is all the way right. The lead and harmony vocals, drums, bass and another electric guitar are all centered. This version sounds hurried.

"I Me Mine": There are lots of differences between this version and the original. First, one of the electric guitars is brought into the center of the mix. Also, a second acoustic guitar playing the chords can be heard on the left, where an electric piano and the harmony vocals on the chorus can also be found. The 12-string acoustic that echoes the melody is all the way right, with harmony vocals, electric guitar and an organ that can be heard only on the third verse. This version has been stripped of the strings and horns that were so prominent on the original mix.

"Across the Universe": A much better version here, with Lennon's voice and acoustic guitar untouched by the phasing effect that marred the original mix. He sounds clearer and more evocative here. A tamboura, played by Harrison, can be heard swirling around the entire mix. The song moves along at a slightly faster clip. Listen to the extra dollop of reverb applied to Lennon's voice during the fade-out. It makes him sound like he's chanting his mantra in the Grand Canyon.

"Let It Be": This version features a completely different piano part and lead vocal. The entire mix is noticeably louder. The backing vocals on both the right and left are much more prominent and have been treated with lots of reverb. The backing vocals go from "oohs" to "aahs" in the last chorus. The electric guitar solo is much more muted here, and less effective. The organ remains on the left, where a Mellotron can also be heard. There is one less chorus on the outro here.

Past Masters Volumes One and Two

ORIGINALLY RELEASED MARCH 7, 1988
RE-RELEASED SEPTEMBER 9, 2009

Past Masters Volumes One and Two are compilation albums comprised of every official Beatles recording not included on their studio albums. It includes A- and B-sides of singles, and a few sundry oddities.

Listening to this compilation provides a keen sense of the hothouse maturation process the Beatles underwent in terms of their songwriting, playing and singing. That it happened within such a short time span makes it all the more remarkable.

These volumes include the British singles the Beatles released that were not included on their albums. The Beatles adopted an unwritten group policy that singles (which were the best-selling pop music format in the 1960s) should not be included on their albums because the listener would then theoretically be paying twice for the same song. It was an incredibly generous philosophy for the band to implement; many artists at the time were perfectly willing to let their fans pay twice for the same song.

The first volume includes the earliest Beatles songs right through to the beginning of 1965, when Beatlemania was cresting. The second volume includes songs from their last couple of singles before they stopped touring, right through to the studios years of 1967–70.

Although the songs on *Volume One* are essential to an overall understanding of the group's career and impact, the mixes are generally pretty uninteresting. A few of the tracks are in mono, and the sonic quality of others is diminished by the limitations of the recording technology available during the time they were recorded. Still, the ebullience and playfulness that imbued the earliest Beatles songs come crashing out of your headphones loud and clear.

It also seems apparent that at this early stage in their recording careers, they were not inclined to go back and clean up little mistakes made during the recordings of the songs. It's unclear whether this was due to limited studio time or their hectic touring schedule. In any case, the mistakes are interesting to listen to, and all of a piece with the imperfections that appear throughout countless recordings during the early years of rock and roll.

Past Masters Volume One

"Love Me Do": The single version included here is the one on which Ringo Starr plays the drums. It's a mono recording and has harmonica, bass, acoustic guitar, drums and all the vocals right smack dab in the center. This version does sound completely different than the version on *Please Please Me* (studio musician Andy White played the drums on that track), with the main differences being that Paul McCartney's vocal sounds a little shaky at times, and the acoustic guitar is way up high in the mix.

"From Me to You": Among the best of the early Beatles songs, "From Me to You" offers a first listen to the inventive harmonies Lennon and McCartney soon became known for. The vocals during the intro are centered, but move to the right for the rest of the song. The acoustic guitar, lead and harmony vocals are on the right, while an electric guitar, bass and drums are on the left. This is the most common mix configuration used on the earliest records. A harmonica and another guitar pair up in the center during the instrumental break. The electric guitar on the left briefly plays the melody line at the end of the song. Lennon's lead vocal is bathed in reverb.

"Thank You Girl": There are virtually no vocals or instruments centered on the mix here; everything is panned. The electric guitar, bass and drums are on the left, and the lead and harmony vocals, acoustic guitar and harmonica are all the way right. Lennon and McCartney commit a lyric flub at 38 seconds in; one sings "would" and the other sings "could." Listen for the heavy echo on the "ohs" during the end of the song.

"She Loves You": This is the sound of Beatlemania in full flower. No other band ever got so much mileage out of the slangy affirmative "yeah." This is a mono recording with a simple complement of instrumentation: Two electric guitars, drums and bass. The lead and harmony vocals jump out of the mix. A minor quibble; Starr is riding the cymbals, causing an incessant hiss that is especially noticeable on a mono recording. As we've discussed, this was a frequent issue during the earliest period.

"I'll Get You": This catchy B-side could have been a hit for another artist. Again, this is a mono recording, with harmonica, two electric guitars, bass and drums. The harmonies are exquisite, as usual, but listen for two mistakes by the singers at 1:13 and 1:16. Handclaps can also be heard.

"I Want to Hold Your Hand": The simple sentiment expressed in the title masks a very complicated song and arrangement. One electric guitar, drums and bass appear on the left, with a second electric guitar on the right. Still a third electric guitar is centered and only plays the simple guitar figure that precedes the third line of every verse. The lead and harmony vocals and handclaps are all centered in the mix.

"This Boy": A beautiful guitar ballad with stunningly precise three-part harmonies, "This Boy" stands as a showcase for Lennon's superb vocals. The acoustic guitar, bass and drums are all the way left, with all of the vocals appearing on the right. An electric guitar is centered, although it sometimes wanders into the left channel (listen for this at 16 seconds in). Another electric guitar appears in the center during the fade-out only. Both the lead and backing vocals have reverb applied to them, and Lennon's solo vocal during the middle eight appears in both the left and right channels. Listen for the obvious edit at 1:27.

"Komm, Gib Mir Deine Hand": EMI's German subsidiary thought it might be a good marketing move to have the Beatles record their two biggest hits to this point in German. The band put up a mild resistance to the idea, but eventually recorded the two songs while they were on tour in Paris. This version of "I Want to Hold Your Hand" is actually in stereo, with the drums, bass and both electric guitars on the left, and all the vocals (plus handclaps) on the right. They recorded the German vocals over the existing backing track of the original song.

"Sie Liebt Dich": For the German rendering of "She Loves You," the band actually had to record a new backing track and vocals, in effect starting from scratch. The backing track on this version is far less inspired, perhaps owing to the Beatles' simmering impatience with the project. All the instruments are on the left and all the vocals are on the right.

"Long Tall Sally": Paul McCartney's love for Little Richard is evident in this faithful rendition of one the latter's biggest hits. McCartney has the center of the mix all to himself, while an electric guitar, drums and bass are on the left, and another electric guitar and a piano appear on the right.

"I Call Your Name": This is a budget version of "You Can't Do That," but still quite enjoyable in its own right. Lennon's doubled lead vocal is centered, along with the cowbell that begins 10 seconds into the song. Again, an electric guitar, drums and bass are on the left, with a 12-string electric guitar having the right channel all to itself. The nice, waltz-like instrumental break returns to the usual 4/4 time signature for the last verse. The doubled Lennon vocal falls badly out of synch briefly on the word "but" at 1:42.

"Slow Down": The electric guitar, drums and bass are again on the left, although the bass can barely be heard at all. A piano appears on the right. The entire mix is bathed in reverb, especially the doubled vocals by Lennon, which share the center of the mix with the lead guitar solo. The scream Lennon lets loose just before the solo sounds almost exactly like the scream he delivered in the fast version of "Revolution" nearly five years later. Lennon muffs a line at 1:14, when it sounds like he sings "girlfriend" and "boyfriend" at the same time. This is a cover of a Larry Williams song.

"Matchbox": This cover features Starr rocking the vocal like he never had before (or ever would again). His vocal is double-tracked and appears in both the center and on the right. Bass, drums and an electric guitar are on the left, with a piano on the right. The guitar solo starts in the center of the mix but moves to the right. Listen for the late appearance of the handclaps two seconds into the song.

"I Feel Fine": The song is introduced by loud feedback from one of the electric guitars, which begins in the center but quickly moves to the right. Five seconds into the song there is the sound of someone accidentally bumping a mike stand in the center. The drums and bass are on the left, with an electric guitar on the right. The lead and backing vocals, superbly delivered by all, are centered, as is the electric guitar solo. Listen for the sound of a dog barking at 2:14 during the fade-out.

"She's a Woman": This is a very untypical song for McCartney; it features a very simple structure and a spare mix. His raw vocal is centered, although he doubles it on the chorus only (this appears in the right channel), and the electric guitar, drums and bass are all the way left. The tricky electric guitar solo by Harrison appears in both the left and right channels. Maracas and a piano part are on the right, although the piano doesn't make its first appearance until the second verse.

"Bad Boy": Another Larry Williams cover, this time performed at breakneck speed. The lead vocal, a tambourine and electric piano are centered, while the drums and bass are on the left. Two electric guitars play the solo, with slightly different performances heard in the center and on the right.

"Yes It Is": A more mature version of "This Boy," with further references to color as a mood indicator (see "Baby's in Black"). This track is notable for the volume pedal guitar Harrison plays throughout, adding a mood-appropriate sighing effect to the song. Drums can be heard in both channels, with the acoustic guitar all the way left. Harrison's guitar and the bass are all the way right. Although the three-part harmony is rendered beautifully, it briefly falls off-key at 1:22 on the word "tonight."

"I'm Down": McCartney screaming again, but this time on a song he and Lennon wrote. The frantic lead vocal, plus some of the backing vocals and electric piano are centered, while an electric guitar, bass and drums appear on the left. The electric guitar solo, which is treated with some echo, appears in both the left and right channels. The backing vocals that emphasize the word "down" are over to the right. The screaming McCartney delivers during the fade-out eerily presages "Hey Jude."

Past Masters Volume Two

"Day Tripper": One side of the best Beatles single of all-time (backed with "We Can Work It Out"), "Day Tripper" is a seriously good, hooky song that it is immediately identifiable to this day by the opening guitar riff. All the instruments and voices are panned, meaning there is nothing in the center of the mix. The riff is played by two electric guitars, one on the left and one on the right. Another electric guitar strums the chords on the left. The bass and drums are also on the left. The bass plays the guitar riff throughout the entire song. The superb lead and harmony vocals are on the right, along with the tambourine. During the instrumental break, as the song surges upward, an electric guitar on the left plays a one-note ascending scale of half steps on each chord change, but flubs on the last note at 1:39. The remastered album corrects the dropouts on the original version of "Day Tripper," which could be heard at 1:50 and 2:32.

"We Can Work It Out": Again, there is nothing in the center of the mix. The acoustic guitar, tambourine, drums and bass are all the way left, with the lead and harmony vocals and a harmonium on the right. It's amazing that these two songs were recorded during the sessions for *Rubber Soul*. Either one of these songs would have been the best song on that album.

"Paperback Writer": There are lots of interesting things going on in the background on this straight rocker. The backing vocals can be heard on the left and right, and the drums and an electric guitar are on the left. The bass is on the right, where an electric guitar makes a brief appearance at :46. McCartney's lead vocal is centered. Listen for a slight sigh at nine seconds in. The backing vocals go wildly off key from 1:20 to 1:22. McCartney makes a huffing sound at 1:45, just before Lennon's high-pitched voice mistakenly sings "paperback" before realizing he came in too early at 1:48.

"Rain": Two loud electric guitars, bass and drums populate the center of the mix here, while Lennon's lead vocal is on the left. A tambourine is on the right, where backing vocals from McCartney and Harrison can be heard only during the verses. Lennon harmonizes with himself during the chorus. The backwards vocal on the fade-out sounds funereal and eerie.

"Lady Madonna": A very interesting mix here, with the piano and drums (played with brushes) on the left, and the bass, electric guitar and a completely different drum part (played with sticks) on the right. The lead and backing vocals are centered, where four saxophones and some handclaps also can be found.

"The Inner Light": Arguably the most obscure Beatles song ever, partly owing to its relegation to the B-side of a popular single, but mostly because of its overly strident lyrics and Indian instrumentation. The only traditional instrument on this track is a harmonium, heard in the left channel. The right channel is awash with all manner of Indian instruments, played by session musicians. Harrison's vocal is centered, and he harmonizes with himself only on the last line.

"Hey Jude": Arguably the best Beatles song, "Hey Jude" was ground breaking at the time and still sounds as moving and operatic as it did when it was released in the summer of 1968. Over a gospel-like piano (the only instrument on the right channel), McCartney delivers one of his best vocals ever. The lead and backing vocals are centered, where a tambourine and occasional handclaps can also be hear978-0-7864-7934-4d. On the left is an acoustic guitar, drums, bass and a 36-piece horn section that gives the 4:02 of anthemic "na na nas" its dramatic sound. Listen for McCartney to say "okay, now" at 2:58, just before the screaming commences. This is an interesting finding. Some people to this day assert that this is Lennon saying "fucking hell," but that is almost hopelessly impossible an assertion to prove. For one thing, the voice that utters the phrase—whatever it is—most assuredly belongs to McCartney. It seems likely, based on its placement in the song, that it was McCartney tipping off his fellow band mates and the extra musicians on the session that this was the point at which the long fade-out was to begin.

"Revolution": One hit of the drums appears in the center of the mix during the introduction, as the heavily distorted electric guitars are heard on the right. They are playing in such close concert with each other, that it actually sounds like a single guitar. When we examine the *Love* album, we'll see that there are actually two heavily distorted electric guitars on this track (easily detected by being separated in the remix of the track). Lennon's lead vocal—doubled at times—is centered, where the lead electric guitar solo and electric piano are also heard during the instrumental break and the outro. Listen for Lennon to sing "evoltution" 22 seconds into the song. Drums, bass and handclaps are on the left. Listen for McCartney to say "wow" 58 seconds into the song.

"Get Back": The single version is stripped of the album's pre- and post-song chatter and gets right down to business. Lennon's lead electric guitar is on the left, and Harrison's rhythm guitar is with the drums on the right. The lead vocal, harmony vocal, bass and electric piano are all centered. The fade-out has the spoken commentary by McCartney, admiring the way Loretta is dressed.

"Don't Let Me Down": This version of this soulful tune is far superior to the version on *Let It Be ... Naked*. It's played more competently and is much slower. The drums can be heard all over the stereo spectrum, and there are two electric guitars, one on the left and the other on the right. The lead and harmony vocals and electric piano are centered, where the very loud bass part can also be heard. Listen as Lennon moves briefly away from the mike and then gets much closer from 2:11 to 2:15.

"The Ballad of John and Yoko": A great track that rollicks along with sonic delights gradually added as the song progresses. Only Lennon and McCartney appear on this track, Lennon handling the three guitars and maracas, and McCartney playing the bass, drums and piano. McCartney also adds a tasty harmony vocal to Lennon's during the middle eight and last two verses. The drums can be heard all over the stereo picture, with the acoustic guitar, lead and harmony vocals and bass in the middle of the mix. One electric guitar and the maracas are on the left, with the second electric guitar and the piano on the right.

"Old Brown Shoe": This is one of Harrison true hidden gems. It's an interesting song punctuated by an incessant slide guitar part, frenetic bass and chugging drums. The lead and harmony vocals and the drums are centered. The electric guitar solo starts in the center but moves left and right. Two electric guitars (including the slide guitar), bass and an organ appear on the left, while the right channel features a piano part.

"Across the Universe": This is the worst of the three versions of this song. It starts out with the sounds of birds (centered at first, then moving to the left) and what sounds like children playing. The brief acoustic guitar intro can then be heard centered and slightly in the right channel (before reverting solely to the center of the mix for the rest of the song). The very hurried lead vocal is also centered. The right channel is populated by an electric guitar with a heavy wah-wah effect on it, inane and totally unnecessary backing vocals, maracas and what sounds like a cello on the fade-out only. Harrison's tamboura can be heard on the left, where two young women's voices sing with Lennon's lead vocal on the choruses. It's puzzling that the band thought to gum up this beautiful song with some terrible ideas.

"Let It Be": A piano (with just a dab of reverb applied to it), leads off the song in the center of the mix, where McCartney's lead vocal and, later, an electric piano can also be heard. The backing vocals start out on the left, but quickly move all the way right. The organ and horn arrangement are all the way left. The drums, bass and maracas are on the right. The electric guitar solo (much less inspired than the one included on the album version of this song) can also be found on the right. Someone says a couple of unintelligible words in the right channel at 1:06.

"You Know My Name (Look Up the Number)": Recording on this comedy lark was begun in 1967, but shelved until 1969, when Lennon and McCartney completed it. This is a mono version. Five separate sections of song—all with a different tempo and style, but delivered with tongues firmly in cheek nonetheless—are stitched together to create 4:17 of head-scratching hilarity. Listen for McCartney to do a great impersonation of an American nightclub singer during the third section of the song. Handclaps, piano, bass, drums, lots of voices and maracas abound. During the last section of the song, a recorder, saxophone and some vibes can also be heard.

The Beatles Anthology

ANTHOLOGY *I* RELEASED NOVEMBER 21, 1995
ANTHOLOGY *II* RELEASED MARCH 18, 1996
ANTHOLOGY *III* RELEASED OCTOBER 28, 1996

> "When you say ["Free as a Bird"] sounds like the Beatles, people may expect it to sound like '65 or '68. It's very similar in some respects to *Abbey Road* because it has the voicing, the backing voices like [in] "Because." But the whole technical thing that has taken place between 1969 and 1995 is such that, you know, it sounds more like now."
> —*George Harrison* [28]

The Beatles Anthology is a massive three-volume collection of alternative takes, homemade demos, rare live performances and a few songs the band recorded but never officially issued. It was released in 1995, along with a companion book and videos. It's a fascinating look into the band's career, from their very early days right up until the break-up (and beyond).

For our purposes, we will only examine 11 songs from *The Anthology*. These are songs that are in various stages of completion that were never released, for one reason or another. The homemade demos, alternate takes of songs that the band did release and the rare live recordings are interesting in their own right, but do not lend themselves well to a discussion of what can be heard on the headphones. Most of the demos consist of just the singer and his acoustic guitar.

There are three songs here that ended up on solo albums after the band broke up: Harrison's sublime "All Things Must Pass," and two McCartney confections ("Teddy Boy" and "Junk"). None of them got the full band treatment, nor were they ever seriously considered for inclusion on a Beatles album.

Any thoughtful discussion of *The Anthology* must include an examination of "Free as a Bird" and "Real Love." These two songs started as demos from John Lennon's solo years. The widow Lennon allowed her husband's former band mates to take these rough tapes and "Beatle-ize" them in the modern studio, in effect creating new Beatles product. The results are both fascinating and frustrating.

"Cry for a Shadow": The only extant Lennon-Harrison composition, "Cry for a Shadow" was recorded in Germany in 1961 during the time the band was backing the ersatz Elvis impersonator Tony Sheridan. It's a bouncy instrumental based around two electric guitars. Lennon's guitar is centered and awash in reverb, while Harrison's lead guitar is on the right. The bass is on the left and the drums are centered. Listen for McCartney to unleash nearly identical sounding screams at 31 seconds, 38 seconds, 42 seconds, 1:32, 1:38 and 1:44. Even at this early juncture, you can hear the development of a tight little rock and roll unit.

"You Know What to Do": All the instruments and voices are centered on this lackluster Harrison composition. Although this shouldn't be considered a finished product by any means, it does have a lead vocal, electric guitar, tambourine and bass. This was recorded at about the time the band was working on *Beatles for Sale*. It's easy to see that Harrison's songwriting chops just weren't up to snuff yet.

"Leave My Kitten Alone": Also recorded during the *Beatles for Sale* sessions, "Leave My Kitten Alone" is a raucous cover of a Little Willie John tune. The lead vocal—treated with heavy ADT—is centered, along with the bass, two electric guitars and drums. The drums leech into the left, where a piano can also be heard. Another electric guitar and piano can be heard on the right. Listen for Lennon to get noticeably closer to the microphone briefly from 1:25 to 1:27. It's possible the band didn't include this on the album because of its obvious resemblance to "Dizzy Miss Lizzie."

"If You've Got Trouble": A Lennon-McCartney original that was given to Starr to sing, "If You've Got Trouble" is a rattletrap of a track, replete with meter issues and poor singing. It was recorded during the *Help!* sessions. An electric guitar and drums can be heard in both the left and center of the mix, with another electric guitar all the way right. The lead vocal, bass, drums, and the electric guitar that plays the solo are also centered. Starr is riding his cymbals with manic delight here. Listen for him to shout "rock on, anybody" at 1:35 just before the guitar solo. That three-word phrase deftly sums up the Beatles' obvious disinterest in this song.

"That Means a Lot": Also recorded during the *Help!* sessions, "That Means a Lot" is a pretty ambitious piece of work that the band never completely pulled off. It has an odd chord sequence and requires the singer (McCartney) to perform some vocal calisthenics not typical during this period. There is a piano on the left and an electric guitar on the right, with the lead and backing vocals, drums and bass in the center of the stereo picture. The whole thing is treated to a dollop of reverb. The best part of the song is the vamping at the fade-out. After discarding the song for their purposes, they gave it to British pop star P. J. Proby.

"12-Bar Original": Recorded during the *Rubber Soul* sessions, this infectious jam features nifty guitar interplay between Lennon and Harrison, while McCartney and Starr provide the rock steady rhythm section. The bass and drums are centered, where a harmonium can also be heard. Two electric guitars are on the left, while another appears on the right, indicating that the song wasn't simply a live studio jam; they overdubbed a third electric guitar.

"A Beginning": A 50-second introduction that was set to either lead off *The White Album* or serve as the intro to the album's coda, "Good Night," this is George Martin at his best. The minor key gives the song a certain dramatic effect, with strings all over the mix, and some brief horns on the left. Ominous and moody, it would have fit in well on *The White Album.*

"Not Guilty": Also recorded during the sessions for *The White Album*, "Not Guilty" would have been Harrison's finest track on that set, had Lennon and McCartney allowed it to make the final cut. Heavy with several crunchy electric guitars and interesting meter changes, it chugs along relentlessly until it ends after an extended guitar workout. An electric guitar can be heard on both the right and the left, while a harpsichord-like keyboard can also be heard on the left. The lead vocal, bass, drums and still more electric guitars are centered in the mix. The song devolves into a weird, waltzy cadence briefly at 1:27. Listen for heavy phasing to be applied to the guitars and Harrison's vocal from 1:35 to 1:44. For all of Harrison's eventual kvetching about being shut out by Lennon and McCartney, it sounds here like the latter two were working hard on this track. The guess is that they didn't want to include a song that dealt so openly with their overbearing behavior toward the youngest Beatle. Still, it's a fine track and would have been among the best on the album had it been included.

"What's the New Mary Jane": This is sort of a "Revolution 9" with a sense of humor. Still, it's 6:12 of almost unlistenable dreck. An acoustic guitar, piano and Lennon's lead vocal are centered, while all manner of pianos, weird percussion, painful caterwauling by Yoko Ono, and odd tape loops swirl from left to right and back again many times. It's unclear whether this "song" was ever intended for official release, or was just a loon for the Lennons' amusement.

"Free as a Bird": Harrison, McCartney and Starr took a poorly recorded master tape of Lennon singing and playing piano, wrote a couple of new bridges, and layered it over with a multitude of acoustic and electric guitars, bass, drums, organ and some beautifully rendered Beatle-esque harmony vocals to turn Lennon's demo into a fully realized song. Lennon's original piano and lead vocal are centered, along with drums, bass, electric slide guitar, and lead vocal parts by both McCartney and Harrison. A brace of acoustic guitars appear on the left and right, as do two electric guitars and all the backing vocals. An organ can be heard in spots on the right. Then, to put the final Beatles exclamation point on the track, the song has a false ending, after which it comes back via a heavy drum part, and a snippet of Lennon strumming a ukulele.

"Real Love": Although "Free as a Bird" was clearly the living band members' choice as the centerpiece of the *Anthology* project, a strong case could be made for "Real Love" being the superior song. Again over-dubbing onto a tape of Lennon singing and playing piano, a plethora of acoustic and electric guitars, new piano parts, and some muscular bass and drums were added to give the song the Beatles feel. Lennon's lead vocal and piano are centered, along with drums, bass and Harrison's exquisitely played electric guitar solos during the middle of the song and during the fade-out. The left and right channels all have the same configuration: Acoustic guitars, piano, electric guitars and backing vocals. Maracas can be heard on the left during the fade-out. A sneaky organ part wafts in and out in the center of the mix.

Love

RELEASED NOVEMBER 20, 2006
ITUNES DIGITAL DOWNLOAD RELEASED FEBRUARY 8, 2011

"[The *Love* album is] really powerful for me and I even heard things I'd forgotten we'd recorded. This album puts the Beatles back together again, because suddenly there's John and George with me and Ringo. It's kind of magical."

—*Paul McCartney*[29]

At first blush, using the Beatles' music as a soundtrack for a Cirque du Soleil show in Las Vegas ran the risk of turning the Beatles into rock and roll's version of Wayne Newton and Sammy Davis, Jr. In the wrong hands, the idea could have become a disaster that might have forever tainted the Beatles reputation as careful stewards of their own songs.

But with Paul McCartney and Ringo Starr (as well as the widows of John Lennon and George Harrison) on board with the idea, the project was handed over to George Martin and his son, Giles, to oversee. What they produced is a tasteful mash-up of the Beatles' music, with snippets from 135 Beatles songs included in the musical mélange.

Not only did they cleverly meld several songs together without making the whole endeavor sound like a cheesy Stars on 45 send-up, Giles freed many of the mixes from their original constraints (created, in large part, by his dad). Songs like "Eleanor Rigby," "Here Comes the Sun," "I Am the Walrus," and "Back in the U.S.S.R." sound transformed by the new mixes. Instruments that were completely buried in the original mixes suddenly come to life, and vocals that were panned too far left or right are given more prominence in the new mixes. This album makes one wish that the same team would apply similar treatment to the entire catalogue.

Almost every sound on this album was created by the Beatles, with two or three minor embellishments. Many of the songs here are truncated by the elimination of a verse or two, principally for reasons related to flow and context. Fitting the guitar and drum solos from "The End" into the introduction of "Get Back" gives one a feel for the Beatles' songwriting sensibilities and their abiding commitment to the quality of their overall sound.

So, what could have been an unmitigated disaster in terms of the potential mishandling of a revered body of work turned into yet another great album of Beatles music. It's especially fun for Beatles fans to listen to on headphones, not only because of the vibrant new mixes, but also because it's interesting to try to isolate each snippet of sound from the vast array of songs from which the producers culled.

The following analysis includes two bonus tracks that were tacked on to the iTunes digital download released a little more than four years after the original release of *Love*.

"Because": The albums kicks off with the sound of birds taking flight (taken from "Across the Universe") before the flawless vocal tracks from "Because" fill your ears. The intervals between lines of the song are extended and filled with the sounds of birds and, eventually, bees. (Get it? Birds and bees on the opening track of an album called *Love*?) The vocals are panned to each side in this mix. The track ends with a crescendo of sound (the three-piano ending from "A Day in the Life," backwards) that segues neatly into the next track.

"Get Back": The universally identifiable opening guitar chord from "A Hard Day's Night" leads into the drum track from "The End," before the guitars and bass from "Get Back" appear in the left channel. During the introduction, a few measures of the guitar solos from "The End" appear (over various crowd noises), before McCartney's vocal from "Get Back" begins. The solo lead guitar is on the right, and the lead and harmony vocals, along with the electric piano, are centered. The track ends (with the last verse missing) with the orchestral swell from "A Day in the Life."

"Glass Onion": The familiar two-hit drum intro to "Glass Onion" introduces the guitar, piano, bass and drums from the original, with acoustic guitar triplets from "Things We Said Today" on the left, and vocals snippets from "Hello Goodbye" on the left and in the center. One line from "Strawberry Fields Forever" appears in the center of the mix, and a sampling of the horn part from "Penny Lane" also makes an appearance. Only a few of the original vocals from "Glass Onion" turn up here.

"Eleanor Rigby/Julia": Backwards vocals usher in the next track, a completely remixed version of "Eleanor Rigby" that doesn't include McCartney's vocal until 29 seconds in. The strings can be heard on both the left and right, as can the backing vocals. The lead vocal appears mostly in the center, but is also doubled in the left and right channels. The effect gives McCartney's lead vocal a bigger, more dramatic sound. There are simply no vocals from Lennon and Harrison on this track. Backwards vocals can be heard centered as the picked guitar chords from "Julia" make their way from left to right, over the sound of some children at play. Then, the sound of an urgent siren appears on the left and gets louder as it makes its way to the right of the mix.

"I Am the Walrus": McCartney giggles one second into this track, and George Martin counts "1–2–3" before the ominous strains of "I Am the Walrus" fill your headphones. The bass, drums and lead vocal are centered, while the strings, harmonium and horns are on the left, with still more strings and an electric guitar on the right. The backing vocals appear all over the stereo spectrum, while the parts from the radio are muted somewhat. There is also a quicker fade on this version. This is one of the songs that is greatly improved by the new mix. The muddiness of the original has been removed, and one can actually hear the drums, bass and electric guitar parts as distinct and vital elements of this song. Lennon's snarling vocal is more prominent.

During the fade, the sound of a screaming concert crowd is brought up in the mix.

"I Want to Hold Your Hand": Ed Sullivan introduces the Beatles, and the opening chords to "I Want to Hold Your Hand" usher in a deft melding of the studio version and the live version from the Hollywood Bowl in 1964. That the two versions nestle so tightly together is more proof that the band sought to recreate their studio songs as faithfully as possible when playing them live.

"Drive My Car/What You're Doing/The Word": The introduction to "Drive My Car" appears and the track kicks off into a mash-up cornucopia of Beatles songs from roughly the same period. The piano and maracas are all the way left, while the electric guitar is positioned on the right. The center is loaded with the lead and harmony vocals, drums, bass, another electric guitar, tambourine and cowbell. The piano and cowbell from "Drive My Car" play throughout the track, even as it segues into "What You're Doing" and, briefly, "The Word." The original guitar solo from "Drive My Car" is replaced with the solo from "Taxman" and sounds completely credible as an alternative. Listen for parts of the horn arrangement from "Savoy Truffle" on the right just before the guitar solo.

"Gnik Nus": Over the drone of an Indian instrument, the vocals from "Sun King" appear here backwards. Even backwards, the harmonies are flawless.

"Something/Blue Jay Way": George Harrison's beautiful lead vocal appears five seconds before the drums come in on this terrific remix of his most famous song. Strings and an electric guitar are on the left, with another electric guitar, organ, piano and additional strings on the right. The piano is much more prominent in this mix. The lead and harmony vocals, bass and drums are centered, as is the exquisite guitar solo. Harrison's lead vocal is much louder and cleaner on this version. At the end of "Something," the strings, organ, bass and drums from the intro of "Blue Jay Way" can be heard. On the right channel, a few of the vocals from "Nowhere Man" can also be heard.

"Being for the Benefit of Mr. Kite": This track starts out sounding much like the original, although the mix is quite different. The bass, much louder in this version, is on the left and the carousel sounds are all the way right. Lennon's much clearer lead vocal is centered, along with the drums, organ and backing vocals. The instrumental break from the original version here morphs into an amalgamation of instrumental parts from "I Want You (She's So Heavy)," and vocal clips from "Helter Skelter," giving the whole thing a much more menacing overall sound, aided by the white noise machine from "I Want You" whirling around the entire stereo picture.

"Help!": This is a fairly straightforward reading of "Help!," with an alternate lead vocal by Lennon. Listen for the tapping on the body of his 12-string acoustic guitar at seven seconds in. That guitar, on the right with the electric guitar, is much louder in this mix. The bass, drums and another electric guitar appear on the left. The lead and backing vocals are centered. The ending is different, with all three voices holding onto the final note much longer.

"Blackbird/Yesterday": Paul McCartney's two most famous songs played in the key of G major on an acoustic guitar are fused together seamlessly here. The acoustic guitar from "Blackbird" is on the right, with the tapping on the left. At 26 seconds in, the song melts into "Yesterday," with McCartney's much clearer lead vocal centered and the strings on the left. The vocal is doubled on the end of the first middle eight only.

"Strawberry Fields Forever": It's fitting that on this track, five other songs can be heard, as "Strawberry Fields Forever" originally underwent so many different permutations itself. It starts out with the original recording (without the ridiculously slowed down lead vocal track), with the lead vocal, acoustic guitar, electric guitar, drums, maracas and horns centered in the mix. Drums and two additional electric guitars can be heard on the left, while the harmony vocals can be heard on the left and right, where still another electric guitar, bass and a doubled lead vocal are situated. During the original version's instrumental fade-out, the piano makes its first appearance on the left. The piano solo from "In My Life" shows up at 1:43, and at 2:40, crowd noises and the horn part from "Sgt. Pepper's Lonely Hearts Club Band" make the scene in the center of the mix, all played over the instrumental track from "Strawberry Fields Forever." The harpsichord part and the strings from "Piggies" arrive at 3:06, and snippets from "Hello Goodbye" appear at 3:27. Slight intimations of "Penny Lane" are woven throughout the fade-out.

"Tomorrow Never Knows/Within You Without You": Over two channels filled with all manner of Indian instrumentation, the familiar sound of the drums and bass (plus the weird chanting) of "Tomorrow Never Knows" appears, with Lennon's heavily reverbed lead vocal intoning a couple of lines from that song. Over that basic track, Harrison's slowed down vocal from "Within You Without You" takes over. It's an interesting idea and works well in this form. The song eventually reverts back to "Tomorrow Never Knows." The chanting continues until one can hear the faint keyboard notes of a familiar song, played painstakingly slowly, until it speeds up into its regular tempo.

"Lucy in the Sky with Diamonds": The lead and harmony vocals, drums and horns are centered, while the keyboard and an acoustic guitar that you heretofore didn't realize was part of this track are all the way left. The bass, electric guitar and organ are all the way right. The lead vocal is much more prominent in the mix (although still speeded up, as on the original mix) and the drums have more bite to them. Over the fade out, the strings from "Good Night" can be heard, which ushers in the next track.

"Octopus's Garden/Sun King": Over the string arrangement from "Good Night," Starr's vocal from "Octopus's Garden" can be heard, but it's slowed down quite a bit to match the plodding tempo of "Good Night." A drum fill ushers in "Octopus's Garden" with earnest in the center of the mix, where Starr's lead vocal, backing vocals by McCartney and Lennon, bass and drums are also placed. An electric guitar and backing vocals are on the left, and another electric guitar, two pianos and still more backing vocals are on the right. Various sound effects from "Yellow Submarine" appear sporadically throughout the track. During the instrumental break, the drum part from "She Came in Through the Bathroom Window" is superimposed onto the left channel. As "Octopus's Garden" comes to its cold ending, the drums, bass and electric guitars from "Sun King" can briefly be heard, before the sounds of rain and thunder make an appearance.

"Lady Madonna": Over laughing voices and a faint piano part culled from "Ob-La-Di, Ob-la-da" that can be heard on the left channel, "Lady Madonna" begins to take shape a few pieces at a time. Over a drum fill taken from "Why Don't We Do It in the Road," the bass and one of the two drum parts appear on the left, where a saxophone soon materializes. The piano and second drum part, along with various handclaps, are on the right. The lead and backing vocals are centered. McCartney's lead vocal is completely different from the one on the original track. The song drifts into a minor key jam beginning at 1:58 that includes parts of "Hey Bulldog," Billy Preston's organ from "I Want You (She's So Heavy)" and Eric Clapton's guitar solo from "While My Guitar Gently Weeps." A sax noodles after the song comes to a cold stop.

"Here Comes the Sun/The Inner Light": This is a far superior version of "Here Comes the Sun" in almost every regard. Harrison's lead and harmony vocals are much cleaner and much louder, as are the two acoustic guitars he played on the original track. Percussion and Indian instrumentation taken from "Within You Without You" can be hard as the track opens, with backing vocals from "Here Comes The Sun" and "Oh! Darling" layered on top of the instrumentation. The lead vocal, drums, bass and handclaps that don't appear until 2:33 appear in the center of the mix, while backing vocals and acoustic guitars can be heard both left and right. The organ and synthesizer are also positioned to the right. After the end of "Here Comes the Sun," the instruments from "The Inner Light" begin, along with some brief vocals.

"Come Together/Dear Prudence/Cry Baby Cry": A straightforward mix of "Come Together" is improved by the clearer quality of the vocals. The bass and percussion are left, while the drums and electric piano are all the way right. The two electric guitars, lead and harmony vocals are centered in the mix. Lennon adds some huffing sounds to the instrumental break on the left, and repeats the word "come" several times. The electric guitar solos that appear in the middle of the song and during fadeout can be heard in the left, center and right of the stereo picture. Listen for handclaps that weren't in the original mix in the left channel beginning at 3:05. Listen for the piano from "Dear Prudence" to make an appearance at 3:14, with other elements of that song also materializing. Then, the "Can You Take Me Back" coda to "Cry Baby Cry" starts playing, where some strings can also be heard in staccato strokes, leading to the next track.

"Revolution": The main revelation on this remix is that the two heavily distorted electric guitars are positioned opposite each other in the left and right channels, distinguishing them from each other in a way that the original mix did not. The lead vocal, drums and bass are centered here, with the electric piano and guitar solos also centered. Both the left and right channels feature one electric guitar and various handclaps.

"Back in the U.S.S.R.": This song benefits from a cleaner sound and from the bass and drums being brought up in the mix. The lead vocal, drums, one electric guitar and bass are centered. The lead and backing vocals are on the left and centered during the middle eight. There is one electric guitar in both the left and right channels, and the piano is all the way right. The guitar solo also appears on the right. The airplane sounds move all over the mix, and there is much more exuberant shouting during the guitar solo and the outro.

"While My Guitar Gently Weeps": George Martin took Harrison's acoustic demo of this song and wrote a stirring string part for it, one of the only instrumental parts on the entire album not created during the original sessions. The acoustic guitar and Harrison's vocal are centered, while the strings first appear on the right, with more strings eventually showing up in the left channel. There is an added verse on this version that didn't make the cut on the original.

"A Day in the Life": A bit of warm-up can be heard, with echo-y acoustic guitar and piano on the right, and with Lennon counting in the song by saying "sugar plum fairy" twice. Curiously, an organ can also be heard on the right during the few seconds before the song begins. The bass, drums and strings are on the left, while a piano, acoustic guitar, maracas and more strings are on the right. The center of the mix features Lennon's lead vocal with lots of echo, and two different pianos. McCartney's vocal—also centered—is delivered completely dry. The ringing alarm clock can be heard right just before the song's crescendo ending, with three pianos simultaneously and emphatically slamming down on the final chord. Listen for the sound of a squeaking piano stool at 4:52 during the extended fade.

"Hey Jude": This version features a warmer (and entirely different) lead vocal by McCartney, and the piano part appearing in both the left and right channels, giving the song a bigger overall sound. The lead vocal, backing vocals, harmony vocal by Lennon, bass, a much louder tambourine and handclaps are centered, with the drums all the way left. The acoustic guitar can be heard on the right. This version is shortened considerably, moving into the final anthemic chorus right after the third verse. "Na na nas" are left and right, while the orchestra is on the left. At 2:54, the instruments (except for drums and tambourines) are eliminated briefly while the singing continues. At 3:07, a much busier bass part joins the action. This bass part can only be heard on the original version of "Hey Jude" during the last few seconds of the fade-out. All the instruments come back in at 3:19, and nothing but the orchestra can be heard backing up the intro to the next track.

"Sgt. Pepper's Lonely Hearts Club Band (Reprise)": This version does not include any crowd noise. Very vigorous maracas can be heard on both channels, while the drums, two electric guitars, vocals and bass are centered. Occasional vocals can also be heard on the left. It sounds like McCartney says "oh, I f——d up" at 1:13.

"All You Need Is Love": This is a beautiful, clear version of "All You Need Is Love," unsullied by some of the sonic gunk that seemed to drag

140

down the original version. The backing vocals here are centered only during the intro, then move to both the left and right. The lead vocal, bass, drums, electric guitar and tambourine are all centered, with horns and various keyboards on the left. More horns, strings and percussion can be heard on the right. Listen for a snippet from "Sgt. Pepper's Lonely Hearts Club Band" to make an appearance on the right at 3:08, and for some of the strings from "Good Night" to appear on the left at 3:14. The song ends with some tomfoolery lifted from their exclusive fan club members-only Christmas messages.

Jolly good, indeed.

"The Fool on the Hill": Over the drone of an Indian instrument, a few bars of what sounds like very tame chamber music can be heard, with piano, acoustic guitar, bass and finger cymbals being the main players. Then, the familiar piano chords of "The Fool on the Hill" start and usher in an uncommonly satisfying alternative take of McCartney's plaintive ballad. The piano, acoustic guitar and drums are on the left, with more drums, another acoustic guitar and a recorder on the right. The center of the mix is filled with the lead vocal, bass, another recorder and three harmonicas. The drum parts heard here do not appear on the original version of this track. A clever little countermelody that makes use of "Mother Nature's Son's" guitar-based melody is added toward the end of the track.

"Girl": This version is different chiefly because the lead vocal is louder and it has a much longer fade-out. Backing vocals and acoustic guitars appear on the left and right, and the left channel also has some maracas. The lead vocal, drums, another acoustic guitar and bass are centered. During the middle eight, a drum part from "Being for the Benefit of Mr. Kite" is layered on top of this track. One quibble: a sloweddown version of the nylon-string guitar figure from "And I Love Her" precedes each of the choruses on this track. It just doesn't seem to quite fit in here.

Still in all, a magnificent end to a fascinating album.

The Mono Albums

"To us, what was important was the balance of the song. We felt we were sort of mixing the message, rather than putting things in places. We just weren't that interested in stereo. It wasn't where we were from."

—*Paul McCartney*[30]

"The very first records we made were mono, though I did have stereo facilities. To make mixing easier, I would keep the voices separate from the backing, so I used a stereo machine as a twin-track. Not with the idea of stereo—merely to give myself a little bit more flexibility in remixing into a mono."

—*George Martin*[31]

It's important to remember that the Beatles, and George Martin, didn't have stereo on their radar screen at the time they created their music in the studio. It wasn't until around 1965 that they even entertained what their music might sound like by placing instruments and vocals in various locations throughout the stereo spectrum.

Still, this is how the Beatles sounded when their music was unleashed on the world. In 1963, the listening public barely had any idea what the term stereophonic meant.

The mono albums, in my view, don't sound nearly as crisp and vibrant as the stereo mixes. There are a few notable exceptions, but in general, the stereo mixes sound cleaner and peppier.

This is especially true on the first five albums the band recorded. It wasn't until *Rubber Soul* that they finally found a way to make mono versions of their songs sound livelier.

As a result, listening to the mono mixes on headphones reveals much less in the way of studio chatter, flubs and vocal oddities. It's easier to bury minor mistakes in a mono mix because all the sound is coming out of the same channels, making isolating certain parts much trickier.

On the first five albums especially, the mono mixes sound muddy, and more often than not the bass guitar part can barely be detected. It's also more difficult to distinguish between the two electric guitar parts that Lennon and Harrison typically played on most of their early songs.

This section examines the mono albums, and will identify sonic differences between the stereo and mono albums. For this section, I listened to the 2009 remastered mono box set, which corrected the various drop-outs and unwanted studio noise that appeared on the original releases. *Yellow Submarine, Let It Be* and *Abbey Road* were never officially issued in mono, so discussions of those albums are not included in this section.

Please Please Me

"To begin with, the Beatles didn't really have much say in recording operations. It was only after the first year that they started getting really interested in studio techniques. But they always wanted to get the thing right so it wasn't a one-take operation. They would listen to it and then do two or three takes until they got it. It was only later on that they were able to afford the indulgence of more time and lots of retakes."

—*George Martin* [32]

The mono version of *Please Please Me* retains most of the feel-good vibe that can heard on the stereo version. This is a testament to the quality of the songs and the talents of the singers. Lennon's cold seems less evident on the mono mixes.

"I Saw Her Standing There": The handclaps are much louder on this version, and the bass retains its prominence in the mix. The electric guitars during the verses are quieter, although during the guitar solo, more reverb has been applied to Harrison's guitar. There is a slightly quicker fade on the last note here.

"Misery": Oddly, it seems like the first chord had already been strummed by the time the engineer potted up the track. Here, there is less of the overbearing reverb on the vocals than can be heard on the stereo version. The piano is a bit louder, and this mix features a slightly longer fade-out.

"Anna": Lennon's guitar is louder and the drums are brought up in the mix. Although the backing vocals are still awash in reverb, the lead vocal is slightly drier on this mix.

"Chains": This is an example of a mono version of a song sounding better than the stereo version. The backing vocals are way up in the mix, and the harmonies sound more in synch when they are lying on top of each other.

"Boys": The fourth song in a row with a one-word title, "Boys" in this version features a slightly louder bass part, and less reverb on Starr's lead vocal. The guitar solo is a little softer on this version. Listen for McCartney's manic scream at :31.

"Ask Me Why": This version has less reverb on the lead vocal, but more prominent harmony vocals. Listen for Lennon to taker the high note on the word "blue" at 1:35.

"Please Please Me": Although this is essentially the same mix that appeared on the stereo album, the bass and harmonica sound a little more prominent on this version.

"Love Me Do": Also the same mix, although the tambourine sounds slightly louder here.

"P.S. I Love You": No detectable difference here, as they used the same exact mix.

"Baby It's You": When the band comes to its first full stop at 10 seconds in, you can hear a lot of residual noise, which is probably the result of the reverb that the vocals are marinating in. The backing vocals are softer in this mix, and the fade-out starts earlier.

"Do You Want to Know a Secret": The only noticeable difference is that the bass sounds slightly louder here. And, while the backing vocals still have the same amount of reverb applied to them, they pulled back slightly on the reverb on Harrison's lead vocal.

"A Taste of Honey": The interplay between the two electric guitars sounds sharper in this mix. The guitars and backing vocals are brought up, and all the vocals are still treated to heavy reverb.

"There's a Place": McCartney's harmony is brought up in this mix, which makes his and Lennon's vocals sound equally loud. In fact, at times the harmony vocal overwhelms the lead vocal. The bass is slightly louder and the harmonica seems to have been treated with a dash of reverb.

"Twist and Shout": This song can't help but sound great in any mix configuration, such is the quality of the performance by the entire band. The guitars are lowered slightly in this mix, and the third harmony during the wordless bridges is lowered significantly.

With the Beatles

"The second album was slightly better than the first, inasmuch as we spent more time on it, and there were more original songs."

—*George Harrison*[33]

The mono version of *With the Beatles* features the worst bass sound George Martin ever applied to any Beatles songs. On a handful of songs, it sounds like there isn't even a bass in the mix. Consequently, many of the tracks have so little in the way of bottom end, which makes them sound hissy and overly trebly. This does not, however, detract from the supreme songwriting craftsmanship that can be heard on most of the originals here.

"It Won't Be Long": The chief difference is that the electric guitars sound louder, and the backing vocals are brought up in the mix.

"All I've Got to Do": There is tons of reverb on the lead vocal here. Having all the vocals sharing the same center of the mix makes this version sound too busy. Although you can barely hear the bass on this mix, a close listen will reveal a bass flub at 1:20.

"All My Loving": The slightly out-of-synch double lead vocals sung by McCartney are more prominent in the mono mix. Again, the bass is virtually non-existent on this track. The wordless backing vocals on the first chorus feature one of the singers delivering a half-note step down, which is not as evident in the stereo mix.

"Don't Bother Me": The claves are louder on this mix, and so are the drums during the fade-out. The electric guitars are fainter.

"Little Child": The harmonica is much louder during the instrumental break on this track, and the cymbals that Starr rides are much hissier here.

"Till There Was You": The chief differences on this song are that the vocal has been brought up in the mix and the percussion is louder.

"Please Mister Postman": A faint electric guitar that is not evident on the stereo version can be heard during the intro. The backing vocals are slightly quieter here. Listen for Starr to deliver a couple of brief drum rolls during the fade-out at 2:31.

"Roll Over Beethoven": This is a perfect example of a mono mix hiding some of the flaws that are more detectable in a stereo mix. The lead vocal synching that clearly Harrison struggled with is essentially buried in this mono mix. Also, the electric guitar solo sounds cleaner and more polished here.

"Hold Me Tight": If there was a bass played on this track, it has been either completely removed here, or totally submerged in this muddy mono mix. The backing vocals sound slightly off-key at times.

On the mono mix, it sounds like McCartney is joining Lennon and Harrison on the backing vocals, something that is not evident on the stereo mix. Listen for McCartney to sing "you-aah" at 1:49.

"You Really Got a Hold on Me": Lennon harmonizing with himself on the verses sounds much better in mono than it does in stereo. The drums get noticeably louder at :25.

"I Wanna Be Your Man": The electric guitars sound busier pouring out of the same channel here. Again, a bass guitar cannot be heard in this mix. Listen for two high-pitched yelps at 1:53.

"Devil in Her Heart": The punched in edit on Harrison's vocal at 11 seconds in, which is so noticeable on the stereo mix, cannot be heard on the mono mix. The chief difference in this mix is that the backing vocals are louder.

"Not a Second Time": The mono mix sounds much more flaccid, chiefly because George Martin's piano part completely overwhelms the lead vocals. Again, no bass!

"Money": Lennon's lead vocal on the first verse sounds a little shaky, as if he was unsure of where to take the melody. He recovers nicely by the time the second verse rolls around. The big differences here are that the guitar comes in earlier on the mono version, and the piano part is slightly different. Also, the screams are much more prominent, and the piano isn't quite as loud during the instrumental break.

A Hard Day's Night

> "So the first year's recordings were made on just two tracks and were live, like doing broadcast. By the time we did *A Hard Day's Night*, we would certainly put the basic tracks down and do the vocals afterwards."
> —*George Martin*[34]

A Hard Day's Night is one of the best-sounding Beatles album in mono. The songs—certainly the best the Beatles had written to this point—retain the pristine quality of their hooks and harmonies in mono, and sound great blasting out of the headphones.

Luckily, the acoustic guitars—played almost entirely by John Lennon on this album—are kept high in the mix, sometimes at the expense of the electric guitars, which sound muted on several tracks here. Once again, the bass can be heard clearly on only a handful of songs.

It's interesting to note that this album does not contain the usual complement of 14 songs; it falls one short of that number. Of the 13 songs on the album, seven of them contain the word "I" in their titles.

"A Hard Day's Night": The opening chord is much louder here, while the cowbell and bongos are quieter. The mono version is hissier, owing to the prominence of the cymbals in this mix. The harmonies sound as exquisite as they do in stereo. The electric guitars are really hidden in the mix, except during the guitar solo. This version has a slightly longer fade, with an elapsed time of 2:35 as compared to 2:33 on the stereo version.

"I Should Have Known Better": This is one of best-sounding mono songs on the album. The acoustic guitar and lead vocal are a little louder, while the harmonica and Harrison's electric guitar part are much quieter. Again, the bass is all but undetectable. Lennon's voice cracks on the word "more" at 1:24.

"If I Fell": The chief differences on the mono version are that the acoustic guitar is not quite as loud and the engineers who worked on the 2009 mono remastered set fixed McCartney's cracking voice on the word "vain" at 1:44. Also, Lennon's lead vocal is single-tracked in mono, but double-tracked in the stereo mix.

"I'm Happy Just to Dance with You": Again, hardly any bass at all. Harrison's lead vocal sounds better in mono, and the bass drum is slightly more prominent in this mix.

"And I Love Her": On the mono mix of this classic McCartney ballad, it's less evident that McCartney's lead vocal is double-tracked. The acoustic guitar is mixed very high, and the nylon string guitar played by Harrison retains its quality.

"Tell Me Why": The mono version of this track sounds almost identical to the stereo version, chiefly because the song has such a low-fi sound to it. The only difference is that Lennon's lead vocal (on the parts of the song when he's not accompanied by McCartney and Harrison) is slightly louder. The vocal glitch that occurs at 1:01 on the stereo mix cannot be detected on the mono version.

"Can't Buy Me Love": The lead vocal on the mono mix sounds muddier than the stereo version. Except for during the solo, the electric guitar is almost entirely absent from this mix.

"Anytime at All": Lots of reverb on the single drum hits that introduce each verse. The piano is much louder here, and there is a quicker fade on the final chord.

"I'll Cry Instead": This is one of the few songs on the mono version of this album on which the bass actually plays a prominent role. The tambourine is much louder here.

"Things We Said Today": For some reason, on the mono mix of this great album track, McCartney's vocals sound much more subdued. Maybe it's because they have to share the same channel as all the clever instrumentation on this track. The acoustic guitar is louder, while the electric guitar is quieter.

"When I Get Home": The lead vocal sounds clearer on the mono version of this song. Unfortunately, the "whoa, I…" part is too loud here and sounds slightly out of tune.

"You Can't Do That": The cowbell is quieter in this mix, but gets louder beginning at 1:54 (right after the guitar solo). The backing vocals are quieter throughout, but especially during the solo.

"I'll Be Back": The harmonies sound great in the mono version, and the acoustic guitar—as it has on the entire album—really drives this song along.

Beatles for Sale

"We were beginning to do a little overdubbing, too, probably a four-track."

—George Harrison [35]

Beatles for Sale is the weakest of the band's first four albums, and the mono version of the album underscores this fact. Uninspired covers (with one exception), and over simplistic instrumentation mar this album and really points out that the band was in a creative holding pattern at this juncture.

Some of the mono mixes sound downright flaccid, without any of the buoyancy and joy that were the hallmarks of early Beatles music. It is recommended that listeners stick to the stereo version of this album. At least some of the mixes on the stereo version add some interesting flavors to an otherwise tepid album.

"No Reply": This version gives the Latin-tinged rhythm a more pronounced reading. The vocals are much louder here, and the acoustic guitar is mixed very high. The piano that can be heard during the middle eight is much quieter on the mono mix.

"I'm a Loser": Here, the backing vocals, bass and harmonica are louder, while the guitars are quieter. This version has a much quicker fade.

"Baby's in Black": This is one of the few tracks on the mono album that sounds at least as good as the stereo version. The electric guitars are quieter during the verses, but the bass drum is louder during the last verse only. The harmonies between Lennon and McCartney sound just as exquisite on the mono mix.

"Rock and Roll Music": Lennon's lead vocal is soaked with reverb, but sounds less imposing when sharing the channels with the backing track. The electric guitars are way down in the mix, and the piano is slightly quieter, except on the final verse.

"I'll Follow the Sun": The percussion is way more prominent on the mono mix, and the acoustic guitar is still mixed just as high. Lennon's harmony vocals are slightly less prominent.

"Mr. Moonlight": The cheesy organ is slightly louder on the verses here, but noticeably quieter during the fade-out. The electric guitars are muted on this version. That annoying squeaking sound can be heard off and on throughout the track. The fade is quicker on the mono mix.

"Kansas City/Hey Hey Hey Hey!": This song—one of the highlights on the stereo version of this album—has been almost completely defanged by the mono mix. The urgency of McCartney's lead vocal is muted, the backing track is really drab, and the electric guitars (except for during the solo) are almost non-existent. Combine these flaws with the fact that the backing vocals retain their overwhelming and over-modulated sound, and you can see how this track falls flat on its face in the mono mix.

"Eight Days a Week": The cymbals and handclaps are noticeably louder here, while the acoustic and electric guitars and the backing vocals are quieter.

"Words of Love": Again, the mono mix on this track relieves it of its overall "big" sound, making it seem tinnier and less interesting to listen to. The bass is slightly louder here, and there is no doubt the harmonies sound great. This version features a slightly longer fade-out.

"Honey Don't": The acoustic guitar is much louder here, while the bass and electric guitar are significantly quieter. Listen for Starr's voice to crack badly at 33 seconds in. He also delivers a spirited "whoo" at 2:36, which is not as prominent on the stereo version.

"Every Little Thing": The last four songs on this album are rendered lifeless by the mono treatment. This great little album track is stripped of its soul by the fact that the mono version has the drums and backing vocals way down in the mix, and the piano is less prominent as well. All the vocals are quieter on the fade-out.

"I Don't Want to Spoil the Party": This song—one of the highlights on the stereo version of this album—doesn't sound very dynamic in mono. The electric guitar is buried in the mix, and the backing vocals are much quieter during the verse. In fact, the lead electric guitar that is so prominent during the intro on the stereo mix is almost non-existent in the mono mix.

"What You're Doing": Almost everything is brought down in the mono mix here: The acoustic is very low in the mix, and the backing vocals are much less prominent during the verses. Even the timpani part sounds smaller.

"Everybody's Trying to Be My Baby": The over-the-top echo and reverb applied to Harrison's lead vocal gives the mono mix an eerie quality that isn't on the stereo version. Like almost every other song on the album, this track has only a hint of a bass sound, giving the song no bottom end to speak of.

Help!

"The 4-track was remote; in those days, it was never in the control room. We had two 4-track rooms where the tape machines were, and there were three studios, so they had to patch them through. ... but eventually they relented. And they sent out six technical staff from the main EMI technical department to supervise the moving of the 4-track machine up the corridor."

—*Geoff Emerick*[36]

Help! is by far the worst-sounding mono album. It's a mishmash of muddy sound, with vocals often being overwhelmed by the instruments, a lot of hiss created by Starr incessantly riding his cymbals and, yet again, almost no bottom end due to the fact that the bass guitar can barely be heard on most of these tracks. The entire album sounds tinny, as if it's emanating from a cheap transistor radio.

It's unclear why George Martin, the band and the record company allowed such an anemic sounding mono album to be released to the masses. They had to have known that it was an inferior product, especially when compare to the high standards they usually applied to everything they released.

Perhaps the constant touring, location work for the film and the breakneck speed at which they were forced to produce music in the studio in the brief intervals between their travels all played a part in this album sounding so bad. If ever there was a candidate for a total remix—even in mono—it's this album.

Help! and *Rubber Soul* were the only two Beatles albums to be released in both mono and stereo mixes simultaneously.

"Help!": The main difference here is that Lennon's lead vocal is completely different than the one on the stereo version of this song. The rest of the track is exactly the same. Here, the drums are muted and the backing vocals are much quieter. The electric guitar figure that is played by Harrison at the end of each chorus totally overwhelms everything in the mix, to the point that you can only really hear the guitar.

"The Night Before": An undercurrent of hiss—aided and abetted by the maracas being much louder—mars the entire track here. The electric piano is also louder. There is hardly any audible bass, and the electric guitar can barely be heard, except during the solo.

"You've Got to Hide Your Love Away": Again, more annoying hiss spoils this version of what is clearly one of the best songs on the album. The maracas, tambourine and 12-string acoustic guitar are louder, although is harder to discern the presence of the second acoustic guitar in the mono mix.

"I Need You": The electric guitar is louder, as are the acoustic guitar and the percussion. Lennon and McCartney's blasé backing vocals still manage to overwhelm Harrison's lead vocal. Listen for McCartney to utter a single indecipherable word at 2:26.

"Another Girl": This song features the best sound they captured on the mono version of this album. All of the vocals sound great, as does the lead electric guitar. Still, there is virtually no low end here. Listen for a slight tapping sound as the song fades out.

"You're Going to Lose That Girl": The spastic congas overwhelm this fun song, even in mono. The electric guitar is much quieter on the mono version and, predictably, the bass can barely be heard.

"Ticket to Ride": It's testament to the outstanding songwriting and playing this song contains that "Ticket to Ride" overcomes the sonic limpness that informs much of the rest of the songs on this album. The drums—the mainstay instrumental part on this track—are even louder here, at times almost overwhelming Lennon's gritty lead vocal. This version sounds as if there is no bass at all on the track.

"Act Naturally": Here, the backing vocals and lead guitar are louder in the mix, while the acoustic guitar is softened a bit. Still, this is another example from the band's early period of Lennon's rhythm acoustic guitar driving the entire band.

"It's Only Love": This is the one track that sounds as muddy in stereo as it does in its mono permutation. They just never quite achieved a good sound for this track. The electric guitar is very loud here, and there is no bass.

"You Like Me Too Much": The electric piano during the intro on this mix is noticeably louder, while the acoustic guitar is much quieter.

"Tell Me What You See": This version is drenched in mud. The tambourine is way too loud, and the electric guitar has been brought up in the mix as well. Listen as the guiro gets louder on the final verse.

"I've Just Seen a Face": On the stereo mix of this song, it's fun to listen to the three different acoustic guitar parts, but on the mono mix, they are much harder to distinguish from one another. The backing vocals and percussion are louder here, and the song seems slightly faster than the stereo version. This is the only song on the album that can be forgiven for not having any low end to it, since no bass appears on the track.

"Yesterday": The strings are much louder on the mono version, and at times they overwhelm McCartney's sublime vocals. The reverb on the middle eights seems more pronounced here.

"Dizzy Miss Lizzie": This fun track is pretty much ruined by the incessant hiss that can be heard throughout its running time. The only notable difference is that the electric piano part is down deeper in the mix here.

Rubber Soul

"The Beatles were always looking for new sounds, always looking to a new horizon and it was a continual but happy strain to try to provide new things for them. They were always waiting to try new instruments even when they didn't know much about them."

—*George Martin*[37]

"Songwriting for me, at the time of *Rubber Soul*, was a bit frightening because John and Paul had been writing since they were three years old. It was hard to come in and suddenly write songs. They'd had a lot of practice. They'd written most of their bad songs before we'd even got into the recording studio."

—*George Harrison*[38]

Rubber Soul is the first of the mono releases to fully capture the distinctive sound of the band as it runs through 14 songs of lasting quality and impact. The tinniness and hiss that can be heard occasionally and (sometimes) frequently on the first five mono albums is all but gone, and the songs sound similar to their stereo counterparts in most every regard. The sonic quality, for the first time, approaches that which they achieved on the stereo albums.

Almost all of the differences between the mono and stereo mix of *Rubber Soul* have to do with running times and a much better bass sound. There are even a few sonic nuances noticeable on the mono version that aren't quite as obvious on the stereo version.

"Drive My Car": The electric guitar and bass are more prominent here, as are the bass and piano during the choruses. The cowbell is deeper in the mix, and the backing vocals are slightly quieter. For some reason, the electric guitar solo sounds less impressive in mono. This version has a slightly quicker fade-out.

"Norwegian Wood (This Bird Has Flown)": The panning on the stereo version is quite off-putting, as Lennon's heavily reverbed lead vocal is so far to the right as to be almost off the scale of the stereo spectrum. Here, there is a lot less reverb on the lead vocal, and the vocal is brought to the center. The bass is louder on this version, although you can barely hear the second acoustic guitar, and the sitar is slightly less prominent, too. The tambourine part on the last bridge is very quiet. This version is three seconds longer than the stereo version.

"You Won't See Me": This song sounds just as low-fi as it does on the stereo version. In mono, the backing vocals and drums are lowered in the mix, while the bass is more prominent and busier sounding. The piano is louder as well. Listen for the loud handclaps during the fade-out.

"Nowhere Man": The lead vocals are still treated with the same amount of over-the-top reverb, while the bass and drums are more muted. The electric guitars (except during the solo) are also lowered in the mix. In mono, the backing vocals threaten to overwhelm the lead vocal at times.

"Think for Yourself": Listen for one second of white noise before the instruments come in at the start of this track. The harmonies sound better in mono, and the fuzz bass and electric piano are louder in the mono mix.

"The Word": "The Word" sounds infinitely better in stereo because the instruments (especially the piano) are panned, leaving more room in the stereo picture for the exquisite three-part harmonies. The bass is less prominent here, giving this version a thinner overall sound. The piano and electric guitar are slightly louder in the mono mix, and the organ is much louder here just before the final chorus. The vocals seemed to have been treated with a little more reverb. The mono version is five seconds longer.

"Michelle": Listen for someone trying to stifle a cough at three seconds into the song. McCartney's lead vocal has a tincture of reverb applied to it here, and the backing vocals and bass are louder in this mix.

"What Goes On": If it's possible, the two electric guitars sound even clunkier, lying on top of each other as they do on the mono version of this track. Conversely, the harmony vocals sound better in mono, although they are slightly quieter here. The lead guitar part during the outro is also missing from the mono mix.

"Girl": Lennon's lead vocal sounds much better in mono, partly because it's mixed much higher here. It's the loudest thing you hear during this song. The backing vocals are slightly higher in the mix, while the inhalation (yes, it's an inhalation and not an exhalation as everyone seems to think) is less prominent in mono. Listen for someone to say "tit" at 57 seconds. Although the mono version starts to fade out sooner, the track itself is one second longer.

"I'm Looking Through You": Almost everything is louder on the mono version of this song: The acoustic guitar, bass, organ and tambourine are all higher in the mix here. Listen for handclaps during the middle eight; they can barely be heard on the stereo version. The mono version is a full seven seconds longer than the stereo version, giving McCartney more time to vamp his vocals on the fade-out.

"In My Life": Not many differences here between the mono and stereo mixes, except that the guitar during the intro is much, much louder in mono. The drums are also slightly louder throughout, while the piano solo is slightly quieter.

"Wait": The mono version of this *Help!* leftover track makes it seem even more out of place on this album. It just doesn't have the same sonic clarity as the rest of the songs on *Rubber Soul*. Here, the percussion and electric guitar are much louder, and the lead vocal sounds slightly clearer. The volume pedal guitar part Harrison plays here is the last of the three times he used it on a Beatles track ("I Need You" and "Yes It Is" being the other songs which featured this quirky sounding effect).

"If I Needed Someone": The chief difference in this mono version is that everything is louder, especially the rhythm guitar part. The bass is also more prominent. Because the lead vocal and the backing vocals are equally as loud, the backing vocals at times overwhelm Harrison's lead vocal part, something that doesn't happen on the stereo version of this track. Listen for lots of very loud percussion during the instrumental break.

"Run for Your Life": This is the only song on the mono version of *Rubber Soul* on which the bass is buried as deeply in the mix as it is on almost every other mono album that came before this. This could have been either a strategic instrumental decision by the band, or it could have just been that George Martin buried the bass part for old time's sake. The lead guitar and percussion parts are much louder here, making the absence of any appreciable low end even more conspicuous. The backing vocals are slightly quieter on the mono mix.

Revolver

"Their ideas were beginning to become much more potent in the studio. They started telling me what they wanted, and pressing me for more ideas and for more ways of translating those ideas into reality ... so they would want us to do radical things, but this time they'd shove in high EQ on mixing, and for the brass they'd want to have a really 'toppy' sound and cut out all the bass. The engineers would sometimes wonder whether there should be that much EQ."

—*George Martin*[39]

Revolver is the first of the mono albums to sound almost as good as its stereo counterpart. It's also more interesting to listen to on the headphones than the previous six mono albums, mainly because there are significant differences in the mixes, and a few wholly different sounds to be heard.

Two notable sonic qualities stand out on the mono mix of this fine album: The bass is finally placed high in the mixes, and almost every sound is louder. There are a few interesting subtleties in the mixes that cannot be heard in the stereo version.

"Taxman": The main differences here are that the guitars and bass are much louder, while the backing vocals are toned down a tad. The cowbell doesn't make its appearance until the 35-second mark. Listen for the extra note being played on the guitar riff during the final verse only.

"Eleanor Rigby": By now, of course, you know that I feel that Paul McCartney is the only vocalist of "Eleanor Rigby." The mono mix of this song does nothing to disprove that assertion. The vocals sound much clearer and cleaner here, chiefly because there is no extreme panning in mono mixes. The vocals are louder, and the double-tracking of McCartney's vocal on the choruses is less evident in mono. The strings (except for the cellos) are quieter on the mono version.

"I'm Only Sleeping": Lots of fun differences to listen for on this one. The acoustic guitar and bass are much louder here, while the clever backing vocals are muted somewhat. The backwards guitar played by George Harrison is much more prominent and can be heard in various additional places during the song. At times, Lennon's lead vocal is overwhelmed by the backwards guitar. There's a longer fade-out here with much more backwards guitar added to the mix. Listen for the last line of the song; it sounds like Lennon sings "I'm only seeping."

"Love You To": Not much different here, although there is a little more of a drone affect on the Indian instruments, and the harmonies sound slightly fuller.

"Here, There and Everywhere": Subtle but significant differences in this mix: The drums are much louder and McCartney's lead vocal doesn't sound as speeded up as it does on the stereo mix. Although both this and the stereo version clock in at 2:25, the finger snaps that are heard starting at 1:55 in the stereo version don't make their appearance until 2:05 in the mono mix, further evidence that they reined in the vari-speed on the mono version.

"Yellow Submarine": The different, more abrupt cold opening to the song sounds rushed and sloppy, especially Lennon's acoustic guitar. The bass is much higher in the mix here, and there are many more nautical sounds throughout the track. The "band" plays a few more notes on this version, and Lennon's echoing of Starr's vocal on the last verse starts one line earlier here. The final chorus is treated with reverb that cannot be detected on the stereo version, and the fade-out is slightly longer here.

"She Said She Said": Not many differences to speak of, except the drums and bass are mixed slightly lower in mono. The organ is more prominent on the verses here.

"Good Day Sunshine": This track sounds great in mono: loud drums and an even louder lead vocal. The layered vocals at the fade-out aren't as interesting to listen to on headphones in this mono version. The drums cut out completely sooner on this version.

"And Your Bird Can Sing": Both the backing vocals and the electric guitar that does not play the catchy riff are louder in mono. The two electric guitars that do play the riff are brought up way high in the mix during the instrumental break. The bass that plays out the song is much louder here, too.

"For No One": The lead vocal is louder and clearer here. The clavichord and, by the way, an acoustic piano are also brought up in the mix. But the main difference between the stereo and mono mixes of this track is that on the mono version, you can actually hear a distinct drum part.

"Doctor Robert": The drums and backing vocals are very muted on this version, but all of the electric guitars, the organ and the maracas are much higher in the mono mix. The cold fade-out is quicker in mono.

"I Want to Tell You": The faded in intro starts much louder in the mono version of this Harrison track. Overall, this is the one song on the mono version of *Revolver* that sounds as muddy as the songs on *Help!*

The very loud piano and even louder backing vocal by McCartney overwhelms Harrison's lead vocal. The track here sounds like it's running faster, and the bass at the fade-out is completely different than the one on the stereo version.

"Got to Get You Into My Life": Everything here is louder, most notably the horns. The lead vocal, bass and the two electric guitars that herald the final chorus are also pushed way up in the mono mix. Listen for the big edit at 2:24, and the much longer fade-out that features completely different vamped vocals by McCartney.

"Tomorrow Never Knows": On the mono version of "Tomorrow Never Knows," fewer tape loops are employed, but they appear in slightly different places: Different sounds are potted up higher at different points in the mono mix. The tambourine is a lot more prominent in the mono mix. The main difference, however, is the drum part: It is much louder and busier sounding on the mono mix here than it is on the stereo mix.

Sgt. Pepper's Lonely Hearts Club Band

"We didn't have a phasing device, so we used to feed back the image and then move it slightly away from the double track. We used to have a vari-speed device which was a bloody great cumbersome box, valve operated, where you could get your two tapes running very closely together. We actually manually altered the speed."

—*George Martin* [40]

"I think what was significant was that we were able to translate images into sound pictures. The lovely thing was that we weren't inhibited. There were no major technical innovations. We were still working on four-track, although sometimes linking two machines. We got round the limitations by subterfuge and ingenuity. We'd already made the major breakthrough which was Artificial Double Tracking."

—*George Martin* [41]

Sgt. Pepper's Lonely Hearts Club Band in mono differs from its stereo counterpart in so many ways that it almost sounds like a whole new album. There are so many sonic peculiarities in the mono version that cannot be detected in the stereo mix.

This is the second album that the Beatles themselves had at least an indirect hand in mixing: That is, they actually supervised the mix (although all final mixing decisions ultimately fell to George Martin and his team). It's interesting to note that the Beatles weren't present during the final mix of the stereo version, this chore at the time still considered a minor nuisance of significantly less importance.

Considering this set of facts, it seems likely that Martin made executive decisions to "clean up" the mono mix by eliminating some of the effects applied to vocals and instruments, changing tape speed here and there, and actually burying vocals or instruments that the Beatles themselves meant for the world to hear.

If this is indeed the case, it's safe to say that George Martin performed this remix surgery with not an ounce of malice. He would have only been thinking to make this masterpiece sound more palatable to the growing tide of listeners who were embracing stereo.

And, it is interesting to listen to in stereo. However, *Sgt. Pepper's Lonely Hearts Club Band* is the only Beatles album that actually sounds better in mono.

"Sgt. Pepper's Lonely Hearts Club Band": The first thing you hear—the crowd sounds—are much louder here, and throughout the song when they pop up. As on almost this entire album, the bass is more prominent. This is a key fact, because Paul McCartney's bass playing has never been as inventive and propulsive as it is here. In mono, it's more difficult to distinguish between the two electric guitar parts. Listen for a completely different electric guitar figure to be played, beginning at 1:54.

"With a Little Help from My Friends": Not much difference here, except that the bass is louder and the last "help" that Starr sings gets noticeably louder at 2:32 to 2:33.

"Lucy in the Sky with Diamonds": Significant differences abound, making the mono version sound almost like a completely different take. Lennon's vocal is treated to heavy doses of phasing throughout, especially on the verses. The Mellotron, backing vocals and bass are all a lot louder, and the tamboura is much more prominent during the verses.

"Getting Better": The strident electric guitar that plays a G chord with a C chord fingering on the eighth fret has a ringing sound to it that sustains itself more clearly during the first verse, creating an almost droning sound. The bass is louder here, although the backing vocals are brought down in the mix. Listen for the tamboura to play a more prominent role on the third verse only.

"Fixing a Hole": Another song with significant differences between the mono and stereo mixes, "Fixing a Hole" in mono has a completely different sounding drum part on the second verse only. The harpsichord, bass and drums are much louder, while the backing vocals—so prominent in stereo—can barely be heard in mono. Except for during the solo, the electric guitar is mixed way down on this version. Listen for McCartney to vamp some completely new (and double-tracked) vocals at the fade-out, especially at 2:34.

"She's Leaving Home": "She's Leaving Home" in mono is really a different song than its stereo counterpart. And why shouldn't it sound that way, considering it's tape speed is a semitone faster, making its elapsed time a full 10 seconds shorter? Somehow, running faster, it doesn't seem so melancholic; McCartney's vocal on the stereo version seems thick-tongued and sloppy, while here on the mono version he seems to be relating a story that really isn't that sad. His vocal has an uplift to it in mono that gives the song a completely different—and more appealing—feel. The vocals are louder in mono, and the strings are potted down a bit.

"Being for the Benefit of Mr. Kite": The chief differences here are the heavier reverb on Lennon's lead vocal (making it sound even more menacing), and the various effects and tape snippets are more prominent, both during the instrumental break and during the final measures.

"Within You Without You": The only real difference between the two versions is the laughter tagged on at the end of the track. In mono, the laughter lasts longer and actually sounds like it has a few spoken words in there somewhere. The mono run time of this song is 5:08, five seconds longer than the stereo version.

"When I'm Sixty-Four": Because the lead vocal is centered here, you can actually here it, whereas in stereo it's panned all the way to the right, giving it a distant, stony quality.

"Lovely Rita": There is a lot more reverb on all the vocals here. The bass, acoustic guitar, drums and piano are also much louder in the mono mix. The weird groans and indecipherable chatter during the long fade appear deeper in the mono mix.

"Good Morning, Good Morning": The crowing sound that heralds this track is louder and slightly different on the mono mix here. While the two electric guitars are deeper in the mono mix, the bass, drums, backing vocals and horns are all much, much louder. The animal sounds during the fade-out are also more prominent in mono.

"Sgt. Pepper's Lonely Hearts Club Band (Reprise)": Like "She's Leaving Home," this track sounds completely different in mono. The guitar figure that leads into it is broken, or at least poorly edited. You can hear two Beatles (Lennon and Harrison) talking over the drum part during the intro, and the crowd sounds make an abrupt appearance at four seconds in, after which you can hear the crowd laugh once again at 11 seconds. Because the crowd sounds are very suddenly introduced into the mix, it makes it sound really fake and contrived, as if it was a quick afterthought. In fact, the entire track has crowd noises, where the stereo version is almost completely devoid of them. The intro is several measures longer, and features as big a drum sound as the band ever managed to create in the studio. The bass is louder, but the electric guitars are buried in the mono mix. Listen for McCartney to deliver some fast-paced scatting, beginning at 1:08 until the end of the song.

"A Day in the Life": The main features of the stereo mix of the best song on the album are that the bass and maracas are much louder during the first two verses of the track, especially during the first orchestral swell. Starr's drums steal the instrumental show here; he's really giving the track a signature sound with his inventive but tasteful fills throughout. For some reason, the vocal "aahs" that bring the song back from McCartney's interlude to its original melody—a dramatic and important part of the song—are much less prominent in the mono mix.

Magical Mystery Tour

"During *Magical Mystery Tour* I became conscious that the freedom we'd achieve in *Pepper* was getting a little bit over the top, and they weren't really exerting enough mental discipline in a lot of the recordings. They would have a basic idea and then they would have a jam session to end it which sometimes didn't sound too good."

—*George Martin*[42]

Magical Mystery Tour in mono sounds a lot less inventive and exciting than the stereo version. The main reason for this is that the songs are so loaded with unusual instruments (for a rock group, that is) that having them pour out of the speakers in mono diminishes the sonic impact of each of the parts. Much of the instrumental color is muted by the mono mix. The songs are still great (well, most of them), but they sound less dramatic in their mono configuration.

"Magical Mystery Tour": The drums and bass are louder in mono, and the lead vocals are slightly overwhelmed by the horns on the first verse. Listen from 1:26 to 1:29 for a blast from the horns that doesn't exist on the stereo version. The guitar on the last verse is mixed higher here, and Lennon's vocal on the last verse has more reverb on it.

"The Fool on the Hill": The lead vocal is much clearer on this mix, and the finger cymbals are slightly louder. The vocals on the fade-out are almost inaudible in mono.

"Flying": The bass and electric guitar are louder, and the acoustic guitar part is more easily detectable in mono. The drums sound way more trebly here. The organ is much louder on the last verse, and the vocals during the last six measures can barely be heard.

"Blue Jay Way": The phasing that is applied so liberally to the vocals here also get all over the drums in mono. The drums sound busier in mono, but the backing vocals can be heard less frequently. Listen for Harrison to harmonize with himself from 2:36 to 2:42. Also, the cello is quieter but pops up in spots on the mono version that differ from the stereo mix. There is a weirder, more discordant ending from 3:43 to 3:48 in the mono version.

"Your Mother Should Know": This song sounds absolutely terrible in mono, mainly because they swathed it with a strange phasing effect that just doesn't work. It gives the entire track a hiss that can't be heard on the stereo mix. The drums are quieter but the organ is much louder.

"I Am the Walrus": The intro is two measures shorter in mono. The cellos are much louder, while the bass can barely be heard. Some of the spoken word parts taken from the radio are much more audible, especially during the extended fade.

"Hello Goodbye": There are not a lot of differences between the stereo and mono mixes of this track, other than the piano being slightly louder on the mono version. Listen for a big inhalation at 2:43 just before the fade-out section begins.

"Strawberry Fields Forever": On the mono version of this masterpiece, the Mellotron is much louder, as are the cellos and horns, especially on the last verse. Beginning with the third verse, the double-tracking of Lennon's vocal is much more apparent. The drums can be heard right away after the song fades and comes back in, whereas on the stereo version the drums don't appear for a couple of measures.

"Penny Lane": Not many differences here, except for the piano being louder and the electric guitar on the last two verses is buried deeper in the mono mix.

"Baby You're a Rich Man": The main difference here is that the handclaps are much, much louder in the mono mix, while the drum part is quieter. Listen for one of the vocals to drop out at 1:45 on the word "one," giving the vocal a slightly flat sound. The fade-out has much wilder vocal vamping in the mono mix.

"All You Need Is Love": The botched guitar solo played by Harrison (listen at 1:27) is slightly repaired by the elimination of the bad notes he played in an effort to rescue the solo that were preserved in the stereo version. Here, the engineers totally potted down that part completely, so that the bad notes cannot be heard. The piano is much more subdued in the mono mix, while the bass is practically buried, until the fade-out.

The Beatles (The White Album)

"I think it was a very good album. It stood up, but it wasn't a pleasant one to make. Then again, sometimes those things work for your art. The fact that it's got so much on it is one of the things that's cool about it. The songs are very varied. I think it's a fine album."

—*Paul McCartney*[43]

"Normally we went to mono first. Up until the *White Album*, they had never been interested in stereo. But they became interested around that time. Paul told me they wanted to make the stereo mixes different from the mono mixes because they'd started to get fan mail about how people were buying both the mono and stereo mixes. Fans were sending The Beatles letters, telling them how the mixes were different. So they realized this was a good way of selling double the amount of albums. So we had to actually make stereo mixes that were different."

—*Ken Scott*[44]

The White Album features the most interesting mono mixes in the entire Beatles catalogue. On almost every song, there are at least one or two stark sonic differences between the stereo and mono mixes. This makes for some great headphone listening.

Once again, the band members were very involved in the final mix-down of these songs. It's also important to remember that George Martin did not produce many of these tracks; he was away for much of the album's recording and left most of the producing chores to his young protégé, Chris Thomas. This could account for the differences between the two mixes.

As you'll recall from our analysis of the stereo version of *The White Album*, very few of the tracks featured contributions from all four Beatles. This tends to give the entire album a sound that reflects the disjointed nature of the group dynamic at that time. Conversely, that's also one of the main reasons *The White Album* is such a colossal musical achievement, and incorporates so many different stylistic flavors.

"Back in the U.S.S.R.": The jet sounds superimposed over this track are more frequent and can be heard in different spots during the song. The bass and drums are buried in the mono mix, giving the entire track a low-fi sound. McCartney's "oh" during the introduction is almost inaudible in mono.

"Dear Prudence": The guitar during the introduction, picked so stridently by Lennon, overwhelms his lead vocal at times throughout the song. This sounds a lot better in stereo.

"Glass Onion": This track sounds great in mono, probably because of the snarling vocal by Lennon and the heavy reliance on its minor key to give the song a certain sonic menace. The tambourine is a lot more prominent in the mono mix.

"Ob-La-Di, Ob-La-Da": The two chief differences here are that the backing vocals are much less prominent in the mono mix, and the handclaps are missing from the introduction.

"Wild Honey Pie": The acoustic guitars are much louder in mono, and there's a whole new layer of vocals added to the mono mix.

"The Continuing Story of Bungalow Bill": Yoko Ono's backing vocals are pushed up in the mono mix, and the acoustic guitar is louder as well. You can still hear someone say "Bill" at 22 seconds into the song.

"While My Guitar Gently Weeps": All of the differences between the stereo and mono mixes of this song occur toward the end of the track. The fade-out lasts much longer in mono, Harrison's impassioned "yeah,

yeah, yeah" is missing from the mono mix, and McCartney's piano part—by any measure one of the highlights of this recording—starts going off the rails at 4:40. Listen for lots of dropout of the track at 4:45, just before it fades completely and segues immediately into...

"Happiness Is a Warm Gun": No other song on the mono version of *The White Album* sounds as different as "Happiness Is a Warm Gun." Frankly, it sounds almost like an alternate take, even though it is not. The lift given to Lennon's lead vocals and harmonies in the mono mix is astounding, and makes for a revelatory listen on the headphones. Listen for a slight tapping during the first two lines of the song, something that cannot be detected on the stereo version. The drums and, especially, the bass are much louder in the mono mix. The bass is so much louder, in fact, that it sounds like a bass part you've never heard before. It gives the track a bottom that the stereo mix just doesn't have. The piano, buried in the stereo mix, is much more prominent here. At the break toward the climax of the song and just before Lennon sings "yes it is," listen for the vocal to get noticeably louder. This is a huge mono-mixing triumph and the best-sounding Beatles song in mono, by a long stretch.

"Martha My Dear": The handclaps are much louder during the instrumental break in the mono mix, but the entire track is plagued by a noticeable hiss that pervades the entire mix. Also, the electric guitar is brought way down in the mono version.

"I'm So Tired": The main difference is that McCartney's harmony vocal is much, much louder in the mono mix. Also noticeable here (but not in the stereo mix), Lennon joins McCartney for harmony vocals on the first bridge only. Lennon's electric guitar is tamped way down in the mono mix, but the bass is much louder.

"Blackbird": The only difference here is that the chirping sounds appear in different places in the mono mix of this track.

"Piggies": The grunting pig sounds occur in different spots in the mono mix, and Harrison's acoustic guitar, capoed way up the fretboard, is much higher in the mix. The harpsichord is louder, but the strings are buried deeper in the mix. If there is bass guitar on this track, it cannot be heard in the mono version.

"Rocky Raccoon": The single cymbal hits come in much later into the song and are appreciably quieter. A drum part that sounds completely different from its stereo counterpart begins at 1:18. The player piano and harmonica are buried in the mono mix. Unlike on the stereo version of this album, there is no time elapsed between the end of "Rocky Raccoon" and...

"Don't Pass Me By": This is a terrible song (and track) by most any measure, but it's even worse in mono. For one thing, it's in a higher key, making Starr's already wonky vocal sound even more tenuous, and the fiddle steps all over the lead vocal throughout the song. In fact, the fiddle part is completely different, especially during the much longer fade, where you can also hear a snippet of cross-talk of the lead vocal faintly in the background at 3:32.

"Why Don't We Do It in the Road": The only differences here are that the piano is much louder in the mono mix, and the handclaps during the introduction are completely missing.

"I Will": The "bass part," voiced by McCartney, doesn't come in on the mono version until 16 seconds into the song (it's there from the beginning in the stereo mix). Maracas make their first appearance at 40 seconds in, and at 1:27, they are shaken vigorously, something that cannot be detected in the stereo version. The harmony vocal that McCartney sang over his lead vocal track can barely be heard in the mono mix.

"Julia": The acoustic guitar is louder in mono, and the double-tracking of Lennon's lead vocal is not as evident in the mono mix as it is in stereo. You can also hear louder inhalations by Lennon at :31 and 2:10.

"Birthday": The vocal histrionics during the drum break are louder and more perceptible, and the heavy reverb on the piano brings that instrument solidly to the forefront of the mono mix. The bass is less prominent in mono, and the vocals are slightly quieter during the final verse.

"Yer Blues": There is a lot more reverb applied to Lennon's lead vocal on the mono mix. You can still hear the clumsy edit at 3:16, right after the guitar solo. The fade lasts a lot longer here, and there is no appreciable silence between the end of this track and the beginning of....

"Mother Nature's Son": The acoustic guitar is louder here, and McCartney's lead vocal has a lot more reverb on it. There is a tapping sound during the wordless choruses that is much more prominent in mono. The brass band's final note holds for a couple seconds longer on this version.

"Everybody's Got Something to Hide Except for Me and My Monkey": The bass is much louder here, and that's a good thing: McCartney's bass part on this track is as inventive as anything on this album and adds an element of tension to the overall feel of the song. At 1:11. Lennon seems to sing "monk-yeah." The crazy fade is even more frenetic in mono.

"Sexy Sadie": The bass gets potted up significantly 19 seconds into this track. The piano is louder here, but the backing vocals much quieter. Listen for a tambourine during the fade that can't be heard on the stereo mix.

"Helter Skelter": There are a lot of differences here: There is far less reverb on McCartney's vocal, at least during the first verse, and the electric guitars are lower in the mix. The whole song sounds like it's moving at a slightly faster clip. The backing vocals in the mono mix are so much louder, especially at 1:54, when Lennon and Harrison sing "yeah yeahs" that briefly overwhelm the rest of the track. When the song comes back in after the pseudo fade, it features a completely different drum part and many added layered sound effects. The mono version is significantly shorter, and doesn't include Starr's complaint about the blisters on his fingers.

"Long Long Long": Not much is different between the stereo and mono mix of this song. The bass and piano are louder in mono, and the second lead vocal by Harrison seems slightly different.

"Revolution 1": This is one *White Album* song that sounds a lot better in stereo, chiefly because the odd positioning of the horns and the wild panning of the vocal during the fade in the stereo mix makes for a much more interesting listen on headphones. In the mono mix the drums are louder and the fade lasts considerably longer.

"Honey Pie": In mono, this song sounds even more like a 1920s-era send-up, which is probably precisely what McCartney intended. His lead vocal is higher in the mono mix. Listen as Lennon's superlative jazz-inflected lead guitar is potted up in the mix, and includes some notes from 1:39 to 1:42 that can't be heard in the stereo mix.

"Savoy Truffle": Both the bass and electric piano are much louder in the mono mix here. The electric guitar, which is considerably louder on the last verse, plays an odd upstroke at 1:50 that can't be heard in the stereo mix. Also unique to the mono mix is Harrison's high-pitched humming at 1:27.

"Cry Baby Cry": The mono mix of "Cry Baby Cry" features lots of delectable nuances that aren't included in the stereo mix. The acoustic guitar is much louder and so is the piano, which can be heard far more often throughout the song, whereas it only appears in selected sections of the stereo mix of this song. The electric guitar is almost completely absent in the mono mix, while the drums are louder. Listen for an organ to enter the mono mix at :40. Lennon sings harmony over his lead vocal at 1:06, and there are weird sound effects added to the mono mix at 1:15. Listen for Lennon's lead vocal to get noticeably quieter during the final verse.

"Revolution 9": This mishmash of tape loops and tortured cater-wauling sounds even less interesting in its mono configuration, if that's possible.

"Good Night": The strings during the intro are slightly different in the mono mix. Throughout the track, the strings tend to overwhelm Starr's earnest lead vocal, which was probably by design. His whispering at the coda of the song is slightly louder.

Past Masters Volumes One and Two

The main difference between the stereo and mono releases of the *Past Masters* set is that *Past Masters Two* has a different running order. The mono version includes the four originals from *Yellow Submarine* (albeit in "fake" mono), and excludes a few songs that were never released in mono ("The Ballad of John and Yoko," "Let It Be" and "Old Brown Shoe").

For the most part, the mono mixes throughout both volumes are not as vibrant as their stereo counterparts. This is especially true on the second volume, which contained songs that the studio-savvy Beatles had loaded with interesting panning techniques and an abundance of instruments. Occasionally, that cacophony of sound can seem overbearing and muddled coming out of the same channel.

Past Masters Volume One

"Love Me Do": This mix is exactly the same as the version on the stereo *Past Masters Volume One*. Refer to the discussion in that chapter.

"From Me to You": The harmonica sounds whinier on this version. The electric guitars are quieter, and there is a lot more reverb on the vocals here. McCartney's harmony vocal is deeper in this mix.

"Thank You Girl": The harmonica can only be heard during the intro and between verses here; it has been excised from the last several measures. While the drums are louder here, the electric guitars are more muted.

"She Loves You": This mix is exactly the same as the version on the stereo *Past Masters Volume One*. Refer to the discussion in that chapter.

"I'll Get You": This mix is exactly the same as the version on the stereo *Past Masters Volume One*. Refer to the discussion in that chapter.

"I Want to Hold Your Hand": Somehow, the drums sound hissier and more trebly in mono. The electric guitars are quieter during the bridges, and the guitar figure heard during the "I can't hide" part in the stereo version is missing here.

"This Boy": The only differences here are that the acoustic guitar is much louder and the drums more muted. Also, it's easier to discern that Lennon's vocals are double-tracked during the middle eight in mono.

"Komme, Gib Mir Deine Hand": The vocals here are louder and much clearer, while the bass is almost nonexistent. The electric guitars are deeper in the mix, and the handclaps, starting at 2:19, are much less prominent.

"Sie Liebt Dich": Here, there is much more reverb on all the vocals, which sound oddly out of synch at times. The drums are really hissy and the electric guitars are quieter. Listen for the guitar flub at 1:48.

"Long Tall Sally": The main difference here is that both the lead vocal and the piano are much louder. The lead guitar is much deeper in the mono mix.

"I Call Your Name": The cowbell begins to clang immediately in this version, while it doesn't appear in the stereo mix until 10 seconds into the song. Lennon's lead vocal is overwhelmed by the drums and percussion in the mono mix.

"Slow Down": The piano is much louder in mono, and the lead guitar is brought way up in the mix during the solo only. The lead vocal is lowered in the mono mix, and has a lot more reverb applied to it.

"Matchbox": What distinguishes this version from the stereo version is that the bass is much louder in mono, giving the song much more forward propulsion. The electric guitar solo is louder, too. The mono version eliminated the handclaps so prominent on the stereo mix.

"I Feel Fine": The vocals are mixed way higher in mono, so much so that the vocals over modulate on the word "glad" every time it's sung. The mono version also has a longer fade-out.

"She's a Woman": The maracas are much more prominent in this mix and the electric guitar has less reverb on it. The piano is almost inaudible in this mix. This mix has a slightly quicker fade-out.

"Bad Boy": The lead vocal has a lot more reverb applied to it, and the tambourine is much more prominent throughout the song. The electric guitar is potted way up high during the solo.

"Yes It Is": The volume pedal guitar that Harrison plays on this track is a much more prominent feature in the mono mix. The acoustic guitar is potted way down low here. The backing vocals during the bridges are louder, and threaten to interfere with the lead vocal.

"I'm Down": All of the vocals are much louder in the mono mix, although the backing vocals are a little less prominent during the fade-out. The electric piano is muted during the first part of the track, but becomes much louder beginning at 1:18. The mono version has a longer and more interesting fade-out.

Past Masters Volume Two

"Day Tripper": Before the signature guitar riff begins, you can hear an annoying tape hiss that is present throughout. The bass that echoes the riff is much louder in mono, as is the tambourine. The third electric guitar that just plays the chords is much quieter here.

"We Can Work It Out": The mono version has a much louder tambourine, and McCartney's harmony vocal during the bridges is louder than Lennon's here. The harmonium is much louder during the brief coda to this song.

"Paperback Writer": The drums, backing vocals and electric guitars are all much louder on the mono mix. There is significantly more "wobble" applied to the vocals at 1:35 until 1:38. This version features a much longer fade-out.

"Rain": "Rain" is spectacularly less interesting to listen to in mono. All of the features that make it such an interesting track are mostly related to their placement in the stereo spectrum, thereby relegating the mono version to the drab and uninteresting category. The bass is louder here and the fade lasts a little bit longer.

"Lady Madonna": The main difference is that the piano is much, much louder in the mono mix, almost to the detriment of the other instruments. It's more difficult to discern that there are two separate drum parts in mono, and the electric guitar is much quieter. Also, the very interesting backing vocals are much deeper in the mono mix.

"The Inner Light": Not much difference here, except that the percussion is slightly less prominent and the lead vocal sounds much quieter.

"Hey Jude": The mono version features a much louder piano throughout the entire song, including during the anthemic jam at the end. The tambourine gets louder on the second verse, just before the drums come in. The acoustic guitar is also louder during the last three minutes of the song. McCartney's exquisite vamping vocals during the long fade are, unfortunately, buried deeper in the mono mix. Listen for Starr to begin crashing the cymbals at 6:50, and then to start playing a faster 4/4 beat at 7:02. The fade-out on the mono mix is longer.

"Revolution": The electric guitar that ushers in "Revolution" is much louder throughout and at times obscures Lennon's lead vocal. The bass is also louder here.

"Only a Northern Song": The four songs from *Yellow Submarine* on *Past Masters Volume Two* are in fake mono, meaning the engineers never created a proper mono mix of the songs. Instead, they took the stereo masters and melded together the two channels into one, creating the illusion that the song was mixed in mono. "Only a Northern Song" sounds almost as weird in mono as it does in stereo, but the placement of all the bizarre instruments in the stereo spectrum make that version at least a little more interesting to listen to. Harrison's double-tracked vocal sounds slightly slowed down in the mono mix. The organs are also louder.

"All Together Now": The bass and acoustic guitar are both significantly louder in the mono mix. Harrison's backing vocal is more prominent in the mono mix. Listen for handclaps beginning at 1:43 that cannot be heard in the stereo mix.

"Hey Bulldog": The biggest difference here is that the drums are much busier in the mono mix. The bass is muted, and the electric guitar solo is buried in the mono mix. This version has a longer fade-out.

"It's All Too Much": A strange feature of the mono mix is that Harrison's lead vocal alternately gets louder and quieter at certain times during the song. The mono mix doesn't sound as "big" as the stereo mix.

"Get Back": This is the final British Beatles single to be mixed in mono. It's got this weird sounding reverb slathered over the vocals and Lennon's guitar solo, which seems counterintuitive to the clean, organic sound the band was going for during the *Let It Be* sessions. The mono version has a slightly longer fade-out.

"Don't Let Me Down": This mono mix is dominated by Billy Preston's electric piano part, which is much louder than on the stereo version. McCartney's harmony vocal sounds clearer here. It's easier to tell in this mono mix that Lennon's lead vocal is double-tracked during the middle eight only.

"Across the Universe": That such a beautiful song received such abusive treatment in the studio is one of the most regrettable musical travesties in the Beatles' catalogue. A truly lovely melody and superlative lyrics are ruined by an electric guitar that has a wah-wah effect applied to it, off-key warbling by two British lasses pulled in off the street at Abbey Road Studios, and wonky backing vocals by McCartney and Harrison. Here, Lennon's clear lead vocal is slightly louder in the mix, but that hardly atones for the puzzling transgressions the band and producer made while recording this song.

"You Know My Name, Look Up the Number": For some reason, a distracting clicking sound can be heard off and on throughout the mono mix of this song. It sounds almost like a mastering flaw, if anything. It cannot be heard on the stereo mix. The drums are much louder here, and McCartney's lounge lizard vocal is brought way up in the mono mix.

Afterword:
"And in the end"

When the Beatles officially announced the band's dissolution in April 1970, it ended eight years of tremendous creativity and prolific output. No other band in the history of rock and roll created such a large body of memorable and lasting music in such a short time. It is an enduring legacy that will be preserved for posterity.

All four of the former Beatles went on to create music during the 1970s that was alternately interesting and often frustrating. Trying to recreate—or at least match—the quality of Beatles music proved to be a daunting, if not impossible, task. It didn't help matters that the listening public expected the same high quality work from each individual member of the group, an almost impossibly hopeless aspiration.

Throughout their solo careers, all four Beatles were laden with two recurrent albatrosses; ongoing group business matters that remained unresolved (and highly incendiary), and rumors of and pleas for a reunion. When asked, as they were incessantly, the former Beatles remained chary on the subject of a reunion. At times, it seemed that they were the only four people on earth who wondered why anyone would want to see them back together again.

John Lennon made two outstanding albums in the early part of the decade—*Plastic Ono Band* and *Imagine*—but the quality of his work thereafter fell off precipitously, mostly due to his own personal demons and his seeming lack of interest in continuing to play the role of rock and roll hero. After five years of staying away from the recording studio, he and Yoko Ono resurfaced with a comeback album—*Double Fantasy*—that was accorded undeserving plaudits, chiefly because of his long exile from the business. And then, of course, he was murdered in New York City—his adopted home—on December 8, 1980.

Lennon's full life was lived in just 40 short years. It seems likely, given the magnitude of his talent, that he would have created more memorable music had he lived. But one gets the sense that he never would have approached the quality he achieved with his long-time songwriting partner, Paul McCartney.

McCartney spent the 1970s releasing a couple of solo albums and then putting together another band, Wings, that achieved overwhelming success. McCartney made more money with Wings than he did while with the Beatles. A massive worldwide tour in 1975 and 1976 (during which he pretty much turned his back on his Beatles past) gained Wings a wide-ranging new audience who hadn't necessarily grown up worshiping his former band. Critics had a field day, however. Not only did he include his wife, Linda, in the band, he made a lot of lightweight and insignificant music that frustrated his fans and music critics, who felt that McCartney was squandering his considerable talents by nestling too deeply in the domestic bliss he and Linda had created together. Only one of his 1970s albums—the exquisite *Band on the Run*—in any way harkened back to the glory days of the Beatles. The decade ended with McCartney serving a harrowing 10-day stint in a Japanese prison, all because he tried to slip a hefty amount of marijuana past the customs officers at the airport.

During the 1980s, McCartney disbanded Wings and set about making some of the worst music ever created by an ex–Beatle. Seemingly content to noodle around in his home studio with all manner of bizarre instruments and even stranger compositions, McCartney's star fell quite a bit during the decade. It didn't help matters much that his 1984 album *Give My Regards to Broad Street* (and the accompanying dismal film which he wrote and starred in) saw him re-recording a handful of iconic Beatles songs, aided and abetted by George Martin. (He did record two excellent albums in the 1980s: *Tug of War* in 1982 and *Flowers in the Dirt* in 1989.)

It was in the 1990s when he hit the road again that McCartney began

174

to restore his slightly tarnished image, this time embracing his expansive back catalogue of monumental hits and providing a three-hour road show that had something for everyone. Even his new music became more muscular and as a result was received more favorably by critics and fans. Macca was back.

As the years rolled on, Linda passed away, and McCartney remarried, got divorced and remarried again. He has been incredibly busy with a wide array of projects—including forays into classical composition, poetry and painting—concert tours and carefully maintaining a high public profile that has kept him in the spotlight. He has achieved a status as one of the greatest composers ever, and the honors and accolades accorded to McCartney have come to him in a steady stream. His productivity is amazing for a man who is in his eighth decade of life.

Still, one gets the sense that McCartney never got over losing Lennon as his writing partner. His musical sensibilities were never as sharp as when he and Lennon were churning out perfectly crafted pop songs at a breakneck pace. McCartney's 1960s output will always outshine his subsequent work.

In fact, the same can be said about Lennon, Harrison and Starr, too. The four Beatles were always better as a unit than they could ever hope to be as solo artists.

George Harrison had a checkered solo career, highlighted by his first solo album, the sprawling and epic *All Things Must Pass*, a triple album consisting of songs that he swept up from the cutting room floor at Abbey Road studios. That they were treated to Phil Spector's over-the-top Wall of Sound production barely hid the fact that only a handful of songs on the album even came close to approaching the quality of "Something" or "Here Comes the Sun."

After that, Harrison released several albums of middling to poor quality, many of which were laden with muddy mixes, poor vocal performances and unmemorable songs, all while espousing Harrison's very particular views on religion and the material world. Most of the public wasn't interested.

The last two albums he released—*Cloud Nine* and *Brainwashed*—contained inklings of his former brio and droll sense of humor. His work with the Traveling Wilburys—a supergroup of his best musical friends:

Bob Dylan, Roy Orbison, Tom Petty and Jeff Lynne—also resuscitated Harrison's image and career.

Sadly, Harrison's last years were not happy ones. In December 1999, a man in the middle of a psychotic episode broke into his home and stabbed Harrison more than 40 times, severely injuring him. Only the quick actions of his wife Olivia saved his life.

Just months after the stabbing, reports surfaced in the news that Harrison was battling cancer. As months went on, it was reported that Harrison had traveled to various locales—Italy, New York, California—seeking the best treatment protocols for his advanced disease. Harrison died in November 2001 after a two-year fight with lung cancer.

Ringo Starr had surprising success in the early years of his solo career. His 1973 album, *Ringo*, served to reaffirm in the public's mind that Starr was a good-time crooner of insubstantial songs, ably assisted by a large coterie of his rock and roll friends. He also occasionally exercised his acting jones by taking small parts in a succession of lackluster movies that made no one forget "A Hard Day's Night."

Over the ensuing years, each of Starr's albums grew progressively disjointed and banal. One could almost hear in the music the substance abuse issues he was having. He and his second wife, the actress Barbara Bach, entered a rehab facility in late 1988 and got sober. In the next two decades, Starr recorded better albums and spent many of his summers touring with Ringo's All-Starr Band, an ever-changing line-up of rock and roll luminaries in various stages of career decline.

With McCartney and Starr being the only living ex–Beatles, a sort of grudging truce regarding all of the Beatle's various business issues was struck. They finally signed off on allowing the band's catalogue to be available for download on iTunes, they agreed to re-release the *Let It Be* album in its original pristine form as *Let It Be ... Naked*, they green-lighted a complete remastering of their entire CD catalogue, and they licensed Beatles songs for use in the Cirque de Soleil stage show called *Love*. They also wholeheartedly approved a Guitar Hero package that included several of their best guitar-based songs.

This is an overly sanguine summation of the Beatles' post band careers. It became eminently clear as the years went by that the Beatles' contributions to music, culture, art and entertainment could never be surpassed by any other rock and roll group. Their impact was too big and too far-reaching. All four of the band members had solo careers that would be the envy of almost anyone else, but it is generally understood in most quarters that they attained much of their solo success by being what they would forever be known as: former Beatles.

But most of all, it all seemed like such fun. Judging from the thousands of miles of film and the seemingly bottomless well of audio tapes filled with between-take studio chatter imbued with an unrelenting cheeriness, the ride the Beatles took through the 1960s seems now like it was filled with thrills, adventure and discovery that only a few very privileged people in this world can ever hope to experience. Almost by osmosis they transferred those thrills to their fans worldwide.

The oft-told story of the Beatles violent splintering from 1968 to 1970 had elements of truth to it, as far as it went. But the almost inevitable break-up of the band failed to hint at the true overarching story: The Beatles were a band that provided happiness for countless millions—through several generations—and the most astounding fact in this equation is that they are still nearly as popular today as they were during the 1960s. That is an achievement that no other entertainment act can claim: not even Frank Sinatra and Elvis Presley, the Beatles' most obvious and proximal cultural descendants.

The break-up also doesn't tell the story of the brotherly love and respect all four Beatles had for each other. Right after the break-up, as we know, all four of the band members, at different times and with varying degrees of venom, used the press to disparage their fellow ex-bandmates. In almost every case, these slurs were strategic and had to do more with ongoing business issues than personal matters between them. As the years rolled on and personal tragedy struck the extended Beatles family on several occasions, they came together to support each other. You know, just like brothers do.

On the occasion of George Harrison's death in November 2001, Paul McCartney was naturally asked by the Associated Press for his reaction: "He was a lovely guy and a very brave man and had a wonderful sense of humor. He is really just my baby brother."

After all they experienced together, it was impossible for them not to be forever swathed in a protective patina of love and respect that only John, Paul, George and Ringo could truly understand.

No other band's music sounds nearly as interesting on headphones as the Beatles'. That is how they intended it to be. Such an aspiration is not on today's popular recording artists' radar screens. The goal today is to make the music sound as loud and catchy as it can to instantly hook the listener, with virtually no thought paid to infusing the music with the sonic nuances that the Beatles strove to include in their recordings. This seems odd in a way: a majority of today's music consumers listen to their music on headphones or earbuds.

It's not an exaggeration to posit that much of today's music will not be played 50 years on because of its obvious disposability. It is massed produced for willing audiences all too ready to throw a new pop hero up the music charts. This isn't a complaint; it's a statement of fact. To have the staying power that the Beatles obviously have, an artist needs great original songs, delivered carefully and recorded expertly.

Listening to the Beatles catalogue on headphones gives the listener the very real sense that the music was made for his or her ears only. It is as if they were speaking a secret language, and letting you—and only you—in on the secret.

Long ago, the Beatles promised "a splendid time is guaranteed for all." And in the end, they certainly delivered on that promise.

Notes to Part Two

1. The Beatles, *The Beatles Anthology* (New York: Chronicle Books, 2000), p. 92.

2. *Crawdaddy! Magazine*, Feb. 1977.

3. The Beatles, *The Beatles Anthology*, p. 107.

4. *The Beatles: Ultimate Album-by-Album Guide*, special *Rolling Stone* edition, 2011.

5. The Beatles, *The Beatles Anthology*, p. 124.

6. The Beatles, *The Beatles Anthology*, p. 160.

7. The Beatles, *The Beatles Anthology*, p. 159.

8. Interview in *The International Times*, Nov. 1966.

9. The Beatles, *The Beatles Anthology*, p. 124.

10. The Beatles, *The Beatles Anthology*, p. 212.

11. Jann Wenner, *Lennon Remembers: The Full Rolling Stone Interviews from , 1970*. New York: Verso, 2000.

12. The Beatles, *The Beatles Anthology*, p. 206.

13. *The Beatles: The Ultimate Album-by-Album Guide*, special *Rolling Stone* edition, 2011.

14. Geoff Emerick, *Mojo* July 2006.

15. The Beatles, *The Beatles Anthology*, p. 252.

16. The Beatles, *The Beatles Anthology*, p. 247.

17. Interview, *Premier Guitar*, July 2012.

18. The Beatles, *The Beatles Anthology*, p. 305.

19. Interview, Radio Luxembourg, Nov. 1968.

20. George Martin and Jeremy Hornsby, *All You Need Is Ears* (New York: St. Martin's Griffin, 1994).

21. The Beatles, *The Beatles Anthology*, p. 338.

22. Geoff Emerick, Musicradar.com, 2009.

23. The Beatles, *The Beatles Anthology*, p. 337.

24. *Disc and Music Echo*, Oct. 11, 1969.

25. *New Musical Express*, 1969.

26. Barry Miles and Keith Badman, *The Beatles Diary* (London: Omnibus, 2001).

27. The Beatles, *The Beatles Anthology*, p. 315.

28. Q Magazine, Dec. 1995.

29. Billboard, Oct. 2006.

30. *Mojo*, Oct. 2009.

31. The Beatles, *The Beatles Anthology*, p. 124.

32. The Beatles, *The Beatles Anthology*, p. 92.

33. The Beatles, *The Beatles Anthology*, p. 107.

34. The Beatles, *The Beatles Anthology*, p. 124.

35. The Beatles, *The Beatles Anthology*, p. 160.

36. Geoff Emerick, interview at mix.com, Oct. 2002.

37. The Beatles, *The Beatles Anthology*, p. 196.

38. The Beatles, *The Beatles Anthology*, p. 194.

39. The Beatles, *The Beatles Anthology*, p. 206.

40. 229 "Sgt. Pepper: The Inside Story," *Q*, July 1987.

41. "Sgt. Pepper: The Inside Story," *Q*, July 1987.

42. The Beatles, *The Beatles Anthology*, p. 305.

43. The Beatles, *The Beatles Anthology*, p. 310.

44. Interview, *Premier Guitar*, July 2012.

Bibliography

Books

The Beatles. *The Beatles Anthology*. New York: Chronicle Books, 2000.

Carlin, Peter Ames. *Paul McCartney: A Life*. New York: Touchstone, 2009.

Davies, Hunter. *The Beatles*. New York: Norton, 1996.

Egan, Sean, ed. *The Mammoth Book of the Beatles: An Anthology of Landmark Interviews, First-Hand Accounts, and Memoirs of the Fab Four*. London: Constable and Robinson, 2009.

Emerick, Geoff, and Howard Massey. *Here, There and Everywhere: My Life Recording the Music of the Beatles*. New York: Gotham, 2006.

Evans, Mike, ed. *The Beatles Literary Anthology*. London: Plexus, 2004.

Evans, Mike, ed. *The Beatles Paperback Writer: 40 Years of Classic Writing*. London: Plexus, 2009.

Lewisohn, Mark. *The Complete Beatles Recording Sessions*. London: EMI Records, 2006.

Martin, George, and Jeremy Hornsby. *All You Need Is Ears*. New York: St. Martin's Griffin, 1994.

Miles, Barry, and Keith Badman. *The Beatles Diary*. London: Omnibus, 2001.

Rodriguez, Robert. *Revolver: How the Beatles Reimagined Rock 'n Roll*. Milwaukee: Backbeat, 2012.

Sandercombe, W. Fraser. *The Beatles: The Press Reports*. Burlington, Ontario: Collector's Guide, 2007.

Scott, Ken, and Bobby Owsinski. *Abbey Road to Ziggy Stardust: Off the Record with The Beatles, Bowie, Elton and So Much More*. Los Angeles: Alfred Music, 2012.

Spitz, Bob. *The Beatles: The Biography*. New York: Little, Brown, 2005.

Wenner, Jann. *Lennon Remembers: The Full Rolling Stone Interviews from 1970*. New York: Verso, 2000.

Magazines and Periodicals

Billboard Magazine
Guitar World
MOJO
Musician
Musician's Friend
New Musical Express
Premier Guitar
Q
Rolling Stone
Shindig
Sound+Vision
Uncut
The Word

Websites

There are countless websites devoted to the Beatles and associated topics. I found the following sites to be full of useful and enlightening information:

beatles.com
beatlesinterviews.org
Mixwww
Rock's Backpages

Index

Index